FOREIGN TELEVISION AND INDIAN YOUTH

About the Author

P. Vijayalakshmi is an Associate Professor in the Department of Communication and Journalism, Sri Padmavati Mahila Visvavidyalayam, Tirupati, Andhra Pradesh. She teaches International Communication, Communication Theory and Advertising. Her research interests include media effects with focus on impact of foreign TV on children and youth, and women and media. At present she is conducting research on "Violence in Televised Cartoon programmes and its impact on children". Her educational background includes Defence Studies from University of Madras; Communication and Journalism from Padmavati Mahila Visvavidyalayam. The University of Pune awarded Doctorate for her research work. She is currently Executive member of Press Academy of Andhra Pradesh. She visited USA, Canada and U.K. under youth cultural exchange programme, sponsored by Rotary International.

FOREIGN TELEVISION AND INDIAN YOUTH
Changing Attitudes

Peddiboyina Vijayalakshmi
Associate Professor
Department of Communication and Journalism
Sri Padmavati Mahila Visvavidyalayam
Tirupati, Andhra Pradesh, India

CONCEPT PUBLISHING COMPANY, NEW DELHI-110059

Cataloging in Publication Data—DK
Courtesy: D.K. Agencies (P) Ltd. <docinfo@dkagencies.com>

Vijayalakshmi, Peddiboyina.
Foreign television and Indian youth : changing attitudes / Peddiboyina Vijayalakshmi.
p. cm.
Originally presented as the author's thesis (Ph. D.)—University of Pune.
Includes bibliographical references (p.)
Includes index.
ISBN 8180690792

1. Foreign television programs—India.
2. Youth—India—Influence. I. Title.

DDC 384.553 208 350 954 21

ISBN 81-8069-079-2

First Published 2005

Published and Printed by
Ashok Kumar Mittal
Concept Publishing Company
A/15-16, Commercial Block, Mohan Garden
New Delhi-110059 (INDIA)

Phones : 25351460, 25351794
Fax : 091-11-25357103
Email : publishing@conceptpub.com

To

My beloved father

Sri P. SOMA RAJU

for his immense love showered on me and for constant encouragement given in every walk of my life. He taught me to respect the human values in life.

Preface

India experienced the sudden and unregulated growth of satellite channels since 1991. India's liberalised policy towards global media affected the domestic media environment in the country. The most important consequence of entry of Foreign Channels is the commercialisation of electronic media in the country. Television, one of the elements of promotion of culture and an instrument to promote development and national identity, is under the pressure of commercialisation. India is now under the pressure of balancing the various goals of information, development and entertainment. At the same time it was also felt that the public broadcasting alone cannot meet the needs of different sections of society by offering variety in programming. As a result, foreign channels continue to attract the Indian viewers especially the urban elite.

At the same time these channels were criticised that these programmes are irrelevant to the Indian audience as they promote alien values. Anxiety was expressed that the implicit values in foreign television programmes set a socio-cultural agenda to its viewers. This issue is widely debated by academicians, research scholars, media practitioners, policy-makers and general public at large. The cultural imperialism theory argues that western values on global media act as a powerful cultural force for local people. The active audience analysts argue that people adopt the Western values according to their needs but do not blindly imitate what they watch on television. Though I don't oppose the presence of foreign television in India, it is very essential to examine the far-reaching implications of foreign television programmes on varied audience. The world societies are moving in a direction to frame appropriate policies to face the competition from the global media and to protect their identity. India is not an exception. The book is an attempt to explore the influence of foreign TV on Indian youth. The youth were particularly taken as they are more vulnerable to the effects of television. Indian society is also in the transition period. The family relations, perceptions about women's role, life-styles and sex norms seem to be undergoing some changes. The book will provide some insights into the impact of foreign television programmes on some of these factors. The book will be of use to those who are interested in foreign media effects. Further the book opens up many issues for further research on the implications of foreign media in Indian context. The book is based on the research conducted for my Ph.D in University of Pune.

The book is based on the research conducted for my Ph.D in University of Pune.

P. Vijayalakshmi

Acknowledgements

I am extremely grateful and immensely indebted to my highly revered research guide Prof. P.N. Paranjpe, Department of Communication and Journalism, University of Pune, for his valuable guidance, critical observations and suggestions on my research work. I specially thank the Professor for patiently and meticulously going through the manuscript of my thesis and offering highly valued advices.

I express a deep sense of gratitude to Prof. H.S. Eswara, Manipal Institute of Communication, Manipal, for the critical comments on my research work and the encouragement given to me throughout the study. His suggestions on the subject are more revealing.

I thank wholeheartedly Dr. Pradeep Krishnatray, Manager—Instructional Design and Instructional Writing, Learning Byte International, Hyderabad for making me to work on SPSS package and thus exposing me to the fascinating world of information technology. His help in carrying out the statistical analysis is of immense value.

I owe special thanks to Sri C.V.S. Sarma, Associate Professor, University of Hyderabad, Hyderabad, for suggesting me a topic on International Communication for the dissertation in my post-graduation. Since then, International Communication has become my passionate area of study. He really extended moral support and breathed in encouragement whenever I was in low spirits.

I warmly thank Prof. V. Durga Bhavani, Head, Department of Communication and Journalism, Sri Padmavati Mahila Visvavidyalayam, Tirupati, who evinced keen interest in the progress of my research work.

I am thankful to Prof. J.S. Yadava, Former Director, Indian Institute of Mass Communication, New Delhi, Prof. Louis W. Hodges, Director, Society and Professions, Washington and Lee University and Washington D.C., Prof. Jay Black, University of South Florida, USA for their ready help when I approached them.

I compliment my brother Srinivasa Rao and my friend Bharati for the invaluable help rendered during the period of collecting and coding the data. I thank the Principals of the colleges in Hyderabad for their cooperation and for permitting me to administer the survey in their colleges. I fondly appreciate the students for actively responding to the questionnaires.

1 profusely thank the authorities of the University of Pune for according permission to bring out my thesis in the book form. Special thanks to Mallik for doing proof reading along with me.

I would like to thank Uma, Aruna, Sandhya and Vijji who remained as my cherished friends. They have always been a source of moral support. I remember my sisters Padma and Jyothi on this occasion for their deep affection and friendship. My husband, Lakshmi, has been a great support throughout the research. 1 offer a deep sense of gratitude to my father Sri P. Somaraju who read the entire script along with me and offered suggestions. 1 owe a lot to my mother Smt. P. Anasuya for the love and support at home which helped me to concentrate on my work.

My little son, Sasank Shouri is thoughtful and understanding and did his own little things when I am involved in my research work. He needs the greatest appreciation.

Tirupati **P. Vijayalakshmi**

Contents

List of Tables

List of Figures

1

Introduction

Media Globalisation: India's Experience

The early 1980s witnessed the globalisation of media all over the world, which gained momentum in 1990s. The new economic, political and ideological environment of the 1980s and 1990s has greatly stimulated multinational companies' cross-border expansion, resulting in a closer integration of the world economy. It is this new stage of global corporate capitalism that has come to provide the basis for the formulation of a foreign media system.

Throughout the world, commercialisation of national television systems has been regarded as an integral part of the economic liberalisation programmes. The rapid expansion of global media has been matched by a rapid deregulation of national television systems and a reduction in legal barriers to cross-border flow of software products. The technological changes such as direct satellite broadcasting dramatically increased the number of channels available in most nations in the 1990s. The number of hours of television watched globally nearly tripled between 1979 and 1991. A 1996 survey (Schroder Wertheim and Co. Report, 1996) of teenagers in TV-owning households in forty-one nations finds that the teenagers watch on an average six hours of television per day and nowhere in the survey the figure is less than five hours.

This has been a boon for the US entertainment industry as it dominates the global market for the production and distribution of television programmes as well as films. Most of the large US-based media firms are in the process of moving from a US-centric production model to an international distribution network model (Landler, 1994). The increasing need for the media giants to localize their content is encouraging them to establish wider international production networks. Another factor in globalising production is the urge to take advantage of lower costs outside the United States.

Richards and David (1996) summarize the process of globalisation in three phases. In the first phase, Lerner and Wilbur Schramm (1967) concentrated on how mass media could be used to speed up development process in a nation. In the second phase, people in the developing countries were suspicious of Western Media dominance which was mainly propagated by the work of Herbert Schiller. In the third phase, developing nations have been caught between two conflicting forces, their resistance to Western media dominance and their need to adapt themselves to the globalisation of media environment.

The contemporary issue in developing nations is their concern about the cultural impact of transnational flows of information and entertainment programmes from the West, especially the USA. There is undoubtedly a heavy one-way traffic in cultural products from the United States to its trading partners around the world. This is partly driven by escalating production costs in the United States and the traditional imperialistic pressure to fund markets abroad (Schiller, 1969; Tunstall, 1977 and Smith, 1980). As US based media giants earn a large share of revenues abroad, they increasingly target different regions and nations of the world, and as a result much of the domestically produced media content around the world increasingly has American flavour.

The commercialisation of global media has taken place, to an extent, at the expense of the previously dominant state-run systems which are now increasingly under pressure. The globalisation of media has resulted in a marked decline in the relative importance of public broadcasting and the applicability of public service standards. Hamelink (1997) states that in response to the trends of globalisation, many countries around the world are revising their communication structures. The strategies in this process appear to become more and more market-oriented.

Another significant development in the process of commercialisation of global media is a radical transformation of the broadcasting structures in many developing countries. The United States displays the model of commercial media towards which other countries are moving. India is no exception. A change in the broadcasting scene in India began in 1991 when CNN started covering the Gulf War, which could be watched only on cable TV. As a result cable TV gained popularity. It is through cable TV that international satellite TV has entered the Indian home offering the viewers unlimited choice. It was augmented by massive marketing strategies of multinational companies and economic liberalisation policies of the Indian Government.

Media have moved to the core of cultural imperialism debate because of their clustering of programmes which includes news, entertainment and advertising and because of their production and dissemination dominated by the multinational corporations of the capitalist world market. Tomlinson (1991) argues that cultural imperialism is more than media imperialism, since the media are not the totality of cultural experiences; they merely mediate capitalist modernity which is a form of global capitalist imperialism. Therefore, cultural imperialism is a far more complex phenomenon, which needs to be studied from various angles.

Entry of Foreign Television Channels and their Consolidation in India

In India, multi-channel television began with the live Gulf War coverage in February 1991 by the American news channel CNN, which was carried by some of the five star hotels in Mumbai and Delhi. They did it primarily for the benefit of American or other foreign guests and affluent Indians. But one has to attribute the credit to CNN for the Live and instant coverage of the United States Forces' action against Iraq. During the Gulf War, people signed up with cable operators in a big way.

The cable industry and satellite channels played mutually complementary roles in the country and gave a big boost to the private television networks. The spectacular rise of cable TV is evident if one examines the growth rate of cable TV operators over the years. The number of cable operators in 1985 stood at 100. At the end of the first quarter of 1991 there were 10,000 operators (Dyal, 1992) and by 1996 there were about 70,000 operators in the country. Some of them had subscriber bases as low as 50 to as high as in the thousands. Most of the networks could relay just 6 to 14 channels as higher channel relaying capacity required heavy investments, which cable operators were loathe to make. American and European cable networks evinced interest, as well as large Indian business groups, who set up sophisticated head ends capable of delivering more than 30 channels. These multi-system operators (MSOs) started buying up local networks or franchising cable TV feeds to the smaller operators for a fee. This phenomenon led to resistance from smaller cable operators who joined forces and started functioning as MSOs. The net outcome was that the number of cable operators in the country has fallen to 30,000 (Indian Television.Com 2004).

The cable operators gradually spread out to many small towns and even some rural areas started receiving satellite channels. Then came the five-channel transmission of STAR TV via Asia sat, the Hong Kong based satellite owned by a consortium of companies. Satellite Television Asia Region (STAR) has multiple channels in its cap since 1991.They include STAR Plus, a channel of serials and English and Hindi entertainment programmes, STAR Sports, a continuous sports channel, STAR News, Channel V and MTV for the young lovers of Western music, and of course BBC. By early 1992 nearly half-a-million Indian households were receiving STAR TV telecasts. A year later, the figure was close to 2 million and by the end of 1995, an estimated 13 million households were receiving cable and satellite channels, making India, the largest market for STAR TV (Sinha, 1998). The British Broadcasting Corporation had an arrangement with STAR for relay of its 24 hour service and began to relay in May 1991. STAR TV took a 49.9 per cent stake in Zee telefilms, the largest private Indian satellite broadcaster. Since then STAR has dominated the Indian cable and satellite TV market reaching 37 per cent of the TV households in India. From September 1991 STAR's other services then began to be seen. Discovery, National Geographic Channel, STAR Movies, Cartoon Network, AXN, Star World, HBO etc., are other additions to foreign broadcasts.

The reasons for the popularity of these foreign channels are many. The satellite channels offer round-the-clock programmes with a wide choice to their viewers. Indian viewers started enjoying this new freedom of choice and came out of the stagnation that they were subjected to by DD's (Doordarshan, Government-owned TV Channel) monopoly for a long period. The viewers can have a cable connection by paying a nominal amount and can watch unlimited number of films, international programmes, sports etc. With the introduction of cable TV, the viewers of different age groups and of different income groups now have an access to different kinds of foreign programmes. The other reason for its success was the leisure at the disposal of the urban people, the money they could afford to indulge in cable viewing and the absence of any DD programme in the late morning and afternoon hours (Bhatt, 1994: 45).

If a family along with children visits a cinema hall, they have to spend on travel expenses, food items and on the tickets, which is expensive to the middle class families. Now with the unlimited number of channels on cable television, inexpensive entertainment is available at home for the entire family. At the same time the programmes on DD lack variety, they are not very attractive and give a lot of space for Government propaganda and social messages as a result, they are quite often drab and uninteresting. In contrast foreign channels have a lot of variety, are full of entertainment are packaged very attractively and aimed at all the members of the people. Moreover their uncensored presentation is found to be bold and beautiful by Indian viewers.

Another reason for the popularity of foreign channels is their live coverage of international events, which were ignored by DD. DD news used to be more Government news full of statements and speeches of ministers and political leaders as well as lengthy coverage of foreign dignitaries to India. It lacked professional approach as a result people were glad when they got news of events rather than statements on BBC and CNN. They also derive vicarious pleasure of visiting foreign lands by watching programme with foreign locales and dealing with foreign lifestyles and behavioural patterns.

Apart from live coverage of major events, interviews with personalities on BBC and CNN, music on MTV, serials and feature films on STAR world and Sports channels attracted both viewers and advertisers which posed a serious threat to DD. The soap operas, talk shows, chat shows, and other programmes have become quite popular among the English speaking homes though these shows promote a very different value system to that of Indians.

Cable has grown without any domestic laws to check or regulate. Moreover the Ministry of Telecommunications, further allows the installation of dish antennas for private viewing, which resulted in an ambiguity in implementation of laws. As a result the cable industry has grown rapidly which poses a challenge to DD. It has broken the monopoly of the broadcasting industry in the country.

Indian Broadcasting was until recent times owned by the Central Government of India. In a democratic set-up, the ministers have to cater to the whims and demands of the politicians in the ruling party as well as the opposition. Similarly Government ownership translates itself in control by the bureaucrats majority of whom are more than willing to bend backwards to keep ministers happy. As a consequence, Broadcasting in India has continuously been under the control of politicians and democrats. The Ministry of Information and Broadcasting is the policy making body for the broadcasting system. The Government finances broadcasting and it maintains a tight control on the expenditure of All India Radio and Doordarshan and the powers of the Director-General. As a result, DD couldn't satisfy the viewers' desire for quality and unbiased coverage. Moreover it offered a limited choice in its entertainment programming.

Television started in India as an experimental service in 1959, and commenced educational broadcasts in 1961. Agricultural programmes followed in 1966 and by 1975 there were six television centres in the country. The real breakthrough, however, came with the Satellite Instructional Television Experiment (SITE) in 1975 under which television programmes received in 2400 villages in six states reached viewers entirely via satellite. With the introduction of colour in 1982, and coverage of major national and international events like the Asian games television grew rapidly from its humble beginnings in 1959 to a commercially viable and strong medium by 1984, when commercials were allowed on television.

At present DD with 1081 transmitters, nearly 50 programme generating centres and 20 different channels puts out 1,393 hours of programmes every week. The terrestrial signals of DD can reach 87.6 per cent of country's 1000 million people (www.ddindia.net). India has an estimated 105 million homes having TV sets (*Times of India*, July 2003). Despite its growth the Indian Broadcasting philosophy was deeply rooted in its commitment to the development process. As a result it was unprepared to deal with the competition from the international channels. With proliferation of channels and increased transmission hours the software requirements of Indian TV channels would be far more challenging to the extent of being detrimental to quality and even to their very relevance. However many feel that DD itself is partly responsible for this situation as it failed miserably to hold the attention of its viewers. Research supported the fact that programmes on DD were not appealing to urban audiences (Singhal and Rogers, 1989). Many a time the quality of DD's programmes in comparison with that of the international channels is questioned. The viewers' preferences have changed a lot and people are now looking for more and more entertainment. Moreover the Government dragged its feet in the case of granting autonomy to Doordarshan for nearly 40 years. No Government had the political will to grant autonomy to DD in spite of the recommendations made by various committees, Chanda Committee (1966), B.G. Verghese Committee (1978), P.C. Joshi Committee (1985) and Prasar Bharathi Act of 1990 and it is only recently that Prasar Bharathi is constituted as an autonomous body. As a result the DD was unable to respond to the competition provided by the satellite channels.

Aftermath of Globalisation

With the advent of satellite transmission, the element of competition has been introduced in the country's entire electronic media. Initially many felt that India is not a major target for BBC & STAR TV and would soon lose their popularity as they reach only the urban people. Moreover only 5 per cent of their audiences know English, the language used by the foreign channels. But most of these foreign channels adapted themselves so quickly to market demand and Indianised their programme contents. They dubbed or sub-titled some of their programmes and telecast programmes run by Indian anchors. Consequently, foreign channels instead of losing their popularity have become more and more popular over the years.

The Government's initial response to CNN and STAR TV took the form of an open skies policy. The reason for the Governments' *laisse-faire* attitude to the onset of broadcasts was its commitment to an open communication system. Another reason is the economic and political circumstances in India when satellite broadcasting was introduced into the country. The years 1990 and 91 were among the difficult periods in India's recent history where she faced one of the most severe economic crises. To come out of this situation, Indian Government opened her doors to the international trade and foreign investment. The cornerstone of the Government's new economic policy was globalisation. As foreign investors closely watch the economic development, "the Indian broadcast policy has become a barometer of its commitment to the reforms" (Sinha, 1998:35). Any attempt to restrict foreign broadcasters would have been construed as evidence of the Government's lack of commitment to opening up the economy. Besides, India is also a member of the International Telecommunication Union, which clearly states that banning a citizen's right to receive TV and radio signals of his/her choice tantamounts to infringing upon his/her personal liberty. Consequently the Government has decided to open up the sky for the foreign TV broadcasters, despite the complaints from many sources about the cultural threat posed by these services.

Criticism was levelled at the foreign TV on many counts primarily for seeming to endanger local traditional culture with unwanted programmes featuring sex and violence. The first and most obvious argument in support of the cultural imperialism approach is that there is a wealth of evidence that cultural tastes and practices are becoming global ones. Take any index, from clothes to food to music to film and TV to architecture and there is no ignoring the sheer massive presence of western cultural goods, practices and styles in every inhabited area of the world (Thompson, 1997). No technology has ever made a so sudden impact on the public mind as that of cable-satellite Television. The satellite TV channels have shown an outstanding growth figure of 500 per cent in the first year, which is amazing (Richards & David, 1996).

With the emergence of STAR TV and other private channels, the whole broadcasting industry has been commercialized. The spread of commercial broadcasting has created a consumer oriented market which further expanded the marketing and advertising infrastructure of the Indian economy which was required for the success of the Government's liberalisation policy.

Emerging Trends in Indian Broadcasting

One of the clear trends seen in the Indian broadcasting is migration of popular and creative directors, producers and broadcasters from DD to these new foreign channels. There might be two reasons for this brain drain. The first and foremost reason seems to be money and popularity. The other reason is that they get more freedom to work in private channels. In the Government media they were always kept shackled. Many programmes have shifted to private channels from DD.

Another important result of media proliferation is the fragmentation of the audience. These channels provide diversity in content and theme targeting at specific groups. There are separate dedicated channels of sports, Hindi films, English films, news services etc. Now more of the Indian Pop stars have been featuring in these channels. The steady Indianisation in terms of content and language of most of the foreign channels gave a further boost to its growth. In the Indian scenario, another trend has been seen aping of successful shows. Many indigenous programmes are just replicas of western programmes, reflecting situations, problems and interactions that are common in the West but are rare in India.

Despite the disparity between Doordarshan (350 million homes) and cable subscribers (40 million homes), a demand is created from the Indian consumer for quality services. However, the total broadcasting industry is in a state of chaos and disarray without any regulatory mechanism. Since the multi-channel network poses a stiff competition, will DD make efforts to get out of its shell? Does the Government want foreign networks catering to Indian TV viewers? Does the Government want to open the skies in a regulated fashion to the outside world or not? It is high time for India to respond to the challenges posed by satellite channels.

Doordarshan's Efforts to Meet the Challenge

The onslaught from the skies in the form of international satellite TV has radically transformed the country's broadcasting environment. The DD responded to the competition on two fronts, by increasing the number of channels and by changing its programming pattern. DD launched its first entertainment channel as first step in 1993, by merging the new second channels that were being programmed by Delhi, Mumbai, Calcutta and Chennai regional stations and networking into a single national channel called 'Metro' or DD2. On 15th August, 1993, the other four channels (business, news, sports and movie) were added to its network. However, DD1 has retained its old identity of being the official media where there was an accent on social educational and developmental programmes. In March 1995, DD launched its International Channel.

DD also revamped its programming of both national and metro networks by involving the private producers. Even news and current affairs which were once regarded as the exclusive domain of DD ceased to be DD's monopoly. The CNN-DD channel agreement even though it failed eventually, reflected a new phase in the transformation of Indian Broadcasting. The old monopolistic attitude was replaced by a more competitive and positive approach.

The whole situation implies that DD has decided to join the race for a share of place in the sky. However, DD is under pressure because it is an official media and is expected to cater to the varied and often conflicting demands from a large social, political and economic groups. The rapid growth of cable networks in both urban and rural areas has made the DD's task of informing and educating masses more difficult, becasue the cable networks supply a continuous flow of entertainment programmes. As a result it has the additional task of providing entertainment to attract and retain mass audiences. Another major problem that the DD experiences is its vast multilingual audiences. Therefore, providing telecasts in regional languages had become a necessity rather than a matter of choice.

Apart from the changed programming strategy of DD, a number of Indian private satellite TV channels were launched between 1991-2000. Some of them include ATN, Zee TV, Zee Cinema, Music Asia, Jain TV etc. Another significant change is the growth of Indian private language channels, other than English and Hindi. Prominent among them are Sun TV in Malayalam, Raj TV, Sun Movies and Vijay in Tamil, Eenadu and Gemini in Telugu, Udaya and Udaya Music in Kannada and Prabhat, Alpha and Tara in Marathi etc. These channels have a large viewership, which accounts for 40 per cent of the estimated cable viewers in the country.

The major changes in DD programming were the result of recommendations made by various committees appointed by Government over a period of time. The committees were appointed from 1991 onwards to look into the various aspects of programming and advertising policies.

The Government appointed K. A. Varadan Committee in September

1991 to examine the idea of offering broadcast rights to reliable organisations in order to provide competition to private organisations. The committee recommended setting up of regional channels. If the scheme had been implemented, the licence would have been granted to private agencies to set up transmitters in towns and cities all over India. The committee had made an alternative suggestion of opening of metro channels to private licensees. It also recommended that broadcasting rights be given to public bodies such as universities and co-operative institutions.

Following the Varadan Committee, Damodaran Committee was appointed to examine the policy implications and the adequacy of existing laws relating to Cable TV and Dish Antenna Systems in the country. The committee recommended the setting up of national authority to license and regulate the growth of cable TV.

Yet another committee Air Time Committee of India was appointed in September 1992 to examine the opening up of the electronic media to private broadcasters and work out the feasibility of giving broadcasting licences to private organisations to broadcast on the second channel of DD and FM radio channels. But the radical recommendations made by the committee were not accepted by the Government.

Responding to the Supreme Court's directive that airwaves need to be freed from Government Control, Sengupta Committee was appointed in 1995. The committee recommended the setting up of an independent Radio and TV Authority of India (RTAI) to regulate the distribution of airwaves by licensing private radio and television channels, domestic as well as foreign and to uplink from the Indian soil. It also recommended that local terrestrial radio stations be permitted particularly because these had competed very successfully with satellite channels in other countries.

Mahalik Committee was appointed in 1996 to make suggestions about what changes are required to be made in the policies and programmes of the electronic media. It made recommendations with regard to contents of DD programmes, the programme scheduling patterns and liberalising the advertising code. The following were the recommendations of the committee:

1. DD should carve out a four-hour entertainment slot in the afternoon targeted at housewives, the senior citizens and children.

2. The national programmes during the prime time should be restructured.
3. The regional centres of DD should be strengthened and made centres of earning advertising revenue.
4. Advertisers should be given advance information about the new and forthcoming programmes.
5. In view of the policy of economic liberalisation, advertising code be liberalised with respect to foreign banks, foreign models and foreign locales.
6. Advertiser should be given volume discount.

Cable Television Networks (Regulation) Act, 1995

All the leading democratic countries in the world have enacted laws on broadcasting, India being perhaps the only exception. The entire cable industry in the country remained technically illegal because the private broadcasting was illegal in India for many years until the Cable Television Networks (Regulation) Act, 1995 was passed.

The bill seeks to regulate the cable industry, makes registration of the cable operators compulsory. The bill says that every cable operator using a dish antenna and television signals receiver shall, from the commencement of the Act retransmit at least one DD channel of his choice through cable service.

Broadcasting Bill, 1997

In February 1995, the Supreme Court delivered a landmark judgement in the case, Ministry of Information and Broadcasting *vs.* Cricket Association of Bengal, which involved the rights of a Cricket Association to give telecast rights to an agency of its choice. Following the judgement on airwaves, the Government worked out a comprehensive broadcast bill in the country. To develop a broadcasting model, media laws in USA, UK, France, Germany, Italy and Australia were studied. The basic framework of our proposed broadcasting bill is therefore based on the relevant UK law.

The Broadcasting Bill, 1997 was enacted to provide the establishment of an independent authority to be known as the Broadcasting Authority of India for the purposes of facilitating and regulating broadcasting services (The Broadcasting Bill, 1997).

The authority would regulate both domestic and foreign satellite TV channels. The idea was to bring private channels, especially foreign networks, within the ambit of Indian laws. One of the conditions for giving licence would be that these networks must uplink from India.

The Broadcasting law covers all aspects of broadcasting in the country including terrestrial broadcasting, satellite broadcasting, Direct-to-Home (DTH), local cable network and unlinking facilities. To avoid the monopolistic tendency, the Bill puts the restriction that a person shall be allowed to hold licence in only one of the categories.

But the Bill does not seem to take into consideration the subtle ideological implications of the news channels. Moreover a special provision in the Bill is incorporated for the reception of unlicensed foreign satellite broadcasting service on the condition that such broadcasting service must be free to air and must not carry any advertisement or carry advertisements for only such duration as may be fixed by the authority and the service is devoted solely to sports, international news and current affairs.

Thus, the last decade witnessed the globalisation of media in India which posed various kinds of challenges to Government Media planners and DD. The various changes brought about in the programming and distribution by DD, appointment of various committees by the Government, implementation of some of their recommendations and enactment of cable bill are some of the attempts made by India to meet the challenge posed by foreign and private Indian TV channels. Whether the efforts succeed or not will be known only by the end of the present decade. But meanwhile the country's youth have been exposed to Foreign Television Programmes (FTPs) for about a decade and will continue to have a choice of FTP in years to come. What will be the shape of media in coming decades and what will be the attitudes of youth to the influence of foreign culture will be decided by the impact that foreign programmes are likely to have on youth of the country today. It is therefore important to study systematically whether the FTP bring about a change in the attitudes of youth towards Western values and lifestyles and whether there is any substance in the arguments put forward with regard to what is known as cultural imperialism.

2

The State of TV Research

Foreign TV and Local Youth

This chapter reviews some of the major studies conducted on Foreign Television Programmes (FTPs) and their influence on various societies. We begin with a review of some pioneering studies about the Television use by youth and proceed to the continuous efforts made to assess foreign TV influence on them.

The phenomenon of television and its influence on youth has been approached from a variety of angles. These studies are broadly divided into three categories. The first section treats some of the notions about television and why and how youth use television. The second part deals with FTP influence on the native cultures with special reference to youth at global level. While reviewing a number of studies on the effects of FTP, it is observed that most of the studies broadly concentrate on the influence of FTP on the purchasing of foreign products, attitudes towards the nation in which these messages originate and stereotyping attitudes towards sender's nations and how these programmes affect their traditional values. The third section discusses the research studies conducted so far on Foreign Television Programmes in the Indian context. A review of these studies is likely to help the researcher to trace the areas which are not dealt by other researchers. It is also likely to help to formulate objectives and hypotheses precisely and clearly.

Television as a Medium for Youth

The impact of TV on the family and particularly on children and young people has been the subject of research ever since TV was introduced. Various studies were conducted to learn how TV was used by the youth.

The task of these research studies was to gain a systematic understanding of youth's way of defining TV and their own experience of TV viewing. A pioneering contribution with regard to TV use came from Surgeon General's study in the USA. The Surgeon General's report (1972) found that there was some relationship between TV use and mental ability. Intellectually brighter adolescents watched less TV and, moreover, were less likely to identify with violent characters. Youth use TV for various reasons. Rubin (1983) identified six television viewing motivations of adolescents: habit, relaxation, companionship, pastime, learning arousal and escape. Rubin explains that television affinity increases with the salience of entertainment, pastime, companionship and information motivations, and decreases with the salience of escape motivation. Perceived television realism increases with the salience of information. Bonafadelli (1986) studies the media functions in the socialisation process of adolescents and states that adolescents use these media to know how other people live and think, to learn things which they don't learn at school, or to learn about new and interesting things. One of the most obvious effects of television was that it was rapidly displacing school activity.

Rogge and Klaus Jensen (1988) studied in the West Germany, the extent to which the TV screen has established itself as a leading medium and viewing habits of youth to determine future patterns of media behaviour. His data identifies the connection between employment and the use of media in families. The psychological burden of unemployment brings stress to the surface of the interrelationship and experience of an unsatisfactory everyday reality geared to reach the media for relief and compensation. All these studies clearly indicate that the youth use television for various purposes.

The pervasiveness and importance of the family has stimulated a wide variety of research throughout the world. Different families use TV for different purposes. By looking into the number of studies conducted in various nations, one can understand how TV is used by the youth in the family, which in turn affects the interaction with other family members.

It was found out that TV sometimes acts as an emotional check for the family members. For instance, Rosenblatt and Cunningham (1976) found greater tension levels in heavier-viewing households and interpreted that these families watch television together as a way to avoid intra family conflict. Lindloff and Traudt (1983) concluded that in higher density families TV viewing might function as a way of avoiding conflicts, lessening tensions in lieu of spatial privacy. According to Johnnson (1983) family life goes on with TV as more or less an integral part of it. Based on longitudinal Swedish data she concludes that TV leads to family interaction and enhances family solidarity especially for children and young adolescents.

A significant contribution comes from Lull (1980). He has generated a typology of the social uses of television following an ethnographic investigation of more than 200 families representing blue-collar, white-collar and farm types. Television was found to be useful to family members for purposes which range from structuring daily activities and talk patterns to far more subtle and involved tasks such as conflict reduction, reinforcement of family roles and intellectual validation as a means for dominating other family members.

Yadava and Reddy (1988) who conducted an in-depth interview schedule on Indian families observed two divergent trends in family interaction as a result of the presence of TV. In some families, there is an increase in the extent and intensity of interaction between members. The reverse is also observed in some other families. Viewers may empathise and identify with characters in programmes and may relate more to the programmes than to the members of their family during the course of TV viewing. Greenberg *et al* (1987) also found that adolescents who live with both original parents watched less television than from single–parent or parent–separated families.

Lull and Se-Wen Sun (1988) also observed some slow and subtle changes in Chinese families wherein traditional orientations towards elder generation and gender were melting away. The active involvement of even very young children in the day-to-day choosing of shows undermines the control of the family agenda permanently exercised by elders. Many families go to bed late in order to watch TV, abandoning the habit of a very early bedtime that has characterised much of Chinese life throughout the centuries. For example, 'KeWang' (Aspirations) was the first Chinese soap opera, the plot of which focused on the aspirations of ordinary Chinese people during the time of the 'Cultural Revolution' (1966-70) and the reform period of the early 1980s. KeWang taught many Chinese teenagers the high value of education, discouraged them from wasting time in discos and bars (Yu, 1991).

Another important work was done by Shanahan and Morgan (1992). They conducted comparative case studies of how adolescents use TV and how this use relates to interactions with their families in five countries, namely Argentina, Taiwan, Korea, China and the USA. Issues addressed include television exposure, family conflict over television and the relationship of TV viewing to family communication. The study indicates a strong positive association between parental co-viewing and their relationship with the parents in Argentina, Taiwan, and USA. The more the students watch with their parents the closer they feel to them and the more satisfied they are with the amount of time they spend together.

Sex role sterotyping in media content has been a major concern of feminist leaders who believe that media images have been partially responsible for creating and maintaining limited social roles for women. We have some support that women interpret TV messages differently from men. For example, female adolescents generally prefer family oriented drama and comedy while males are heavy viewers of action, adventure and sports.

We also have support for the argument that women perceptions about life and their own identity are influenced by the way women characters are portrayed. Adolescents are believed to be particularly vulnerable to the thin-promoting messages of the thin ideals because they are at a time in their lives when they are seeking outside information to form self-identity. Harrison and Cantor (1997) applied social learning theory in a study of college students to examine the separate impact of magazine and television exposure on body image disturbance. They found out that overall TV viewing related to body dissatisfaction but not to a drive for thinness or eating disorder behaviour. Botta (1999) conducted a research on 214 high school girls to predict adolescents' body image disturbance and thin ideal endorsement. Media variables accounted for 15 per cent of the variance for drive for thinness, 17 per cent for body dissatisfaction, 16 per cent for bulimic behaviour and 33 per cent for their ideal endorsement.

Researchers have found that popular music plays an important role in adolescent's sub-cultures and subsequent socialisation to the mainstream culture. Music does not just represent sub-cultures but actively constructs them.

Many claimed to use music for emotional management, either mood enhancing (energising, strengthening or lifting) or tranquillising.

Overall, it is clear that for many adolescents who like popular music, it is a powerful tool for expressing and managing emotions. Mood Management theory eloquently addresses the psychological choices of music of the regulation and management of emotional status (Zillman, 1988). Melton and Galician (1987) consciously employed uses and gratifications approach to study the use of music videos among the adolescents. They found that respondents felt that music videos provided need satisfaction, mood shifting and forgetting about problems.

The early study of MTV video suggested that viewers consider music videos more favourably and as more active and potent than the audio version of the same songs (Rubin *et al.* 1986). Brown and Kenneth (1986) found that music videos have become an important part of American adolescents pattern of media use. According to the research, adolescents watch music videos primarily for diversion. To them videos are exciting; they are a good thing to do when alone and they get the adolescents the mood they like to be in.

In another study, Rogge *et al.* (1988) found that adolescents seek loud pop music when they have quarrelled with their parents. In another study, it was found that music performs mainly emotional functions for adolescents. It is used by youngsters in Switzerland as a means to control moods and to cope up with tensions (Bonafadelli, 1986).

Emotional use of music was related to social variables like gender, grades in school, ethnic differences etc. Women tend to associate emotions with music more than men. Wells and Ernest (1991) found that women choose songs that express hope, happiness, passion and grief slightly more than men. Men were more likely to choose excitement, delight, anger and hate. The ethnic group to which they belong to also influences the viewing patterns of music (Brown, *et al.* 1986). American adolescents watch music videos primarily for diversion and black males and black and white females were more likely than white males say they are using music videos as a social stimulus and to learn the latest dances and fashions. It is something to do or talk about with friends. Blacks were also more likely than whites to report that they use music videos as a school of life and because they wish they were like people in the videos.

Adolescents also use music videos for stimulation or support in social situations indicating they are serving a role in adolescent peer interaction. Adolescents sometimes identify with themes and values projected in the music videos. Research indicates that viewers can be affected by the content of the videos they watch. Typically, viewers show increased liking for the kinds of behaviours they have just seen in music videos. In one study with the college students, it was found that even a brief exposure to rock music videos with sex-role stereotypical or anti-social themes alters viewers' social judgements, modifying their impressions and evaluations of real people. They also observed students performing behaviours similar to those in the videos (Hansen, 1989 and Hansen & Hansen, 1990).

The music videos have been criticized over the years for the large doses of violence, sexuality, anti-social behaviour and patriarchal nature/stereotypical images of women both in the lyrics and visual contents of music videos. Even research of 10 years on music videos indicate that the content is full of stereotyped sex role (Vincent *et al.*, 1987). Sherman and Dominick (1986) found that women were presented as submissive, passive, physically attractive and sensual. The rapid growth of the new musical genre can be tied directly to the rise of satellite television channels (or) services like MTV (music television) and STAR TV music programmes have carved out a permanent niche in the electronic psyche of teen and young adult audiences. There is no controversial but surprisingly, there is still scant published evidence documenting the effect of these music videos on their audience in Indian context.

Foreign Television and Youth: Global Experience

The passing of the cold war era has led to a relatively calm international political climate and the rapid development of communication technology. Mohammadi (1997) identifies two major global trends that are currently shaping the future of the world; the wide proliferation of modern communication and information technologies and the increasing democratisation of social systems around the world. We may add a third trend; the rapid global expansion of multinational media corporations and the culture they promote in the third world countries. Popular culture for instance, has become America's second biggest export after the aircraft industry (*New York Times*, 1994 : 1).

Most of the media imperialism literature appeared in the 1970s. Schiller (1969), one of the main proponents of the theory of media imperialism, is sharply critical of the Western media. He sees the Western media as a powerful force in transforming people's social behaviour and their dreams.

Research groups, after experiencing the consumer culture promoted by multinational companies, were soon giving their attention to document the effects of US corporate expansion into the domain of the third world media systems, advertisements and markets. An important European contribution in the early 1970s came from Tapio Varis in Scandinavia. Based on questionnaire responses by programmers in more than fifty countries, this study documents the structure of programming categories, the percentage and source of imported material and the directions of the international flow of programming on TV evidencing the dominance of the US and European countries (Varis, 1984).

Similarly, Latin American communication researchers began to analyze the nature and perceived effects of the rapid spread of mass media particularly commercial TV as a foreign cultural influence in their region. Before the early 1970s and 80s, a good deal of attention in Latin American communication writing was focused on critical analysis of the media but with relatively little attention to audiences (McAnany and Antonio, 1986). Later, emphasis was laid on media and audiences by exploring what popular culture meant for Latin American audiences (McAnany and Antonio, 1994).

The amount of time of exposure to programmes on foreign channels and its impact on the society has been one of the major concerns all over the world. The impact of TV's incessant presentation of social roles is sometimes a problem for cultures that differ in their values from the place where these programmes originate. Ideas about family, marriage, love and romance are not the same as projected in foreign programmes as they are within the country. We will review some of the experiences of other nations in the following sections.

An important contribution of FTP influence has come from Kang and Michael Morgan (1988). Their study confirms the impact of American Forces' Korean Network (AFKN) on Korean family system. AFKN was the channel focused in the research because it broadcast US programmes and Korean officials played virtually no role in its programming. A study on the college students of Korea was conducted. A self-administered questionnaire was given to 226 Korean college students in Seoul, Korea. Family norms vary according to cultural standards prevailing in the society. Obeying one's parents is the central tenet of the Korean family system. They concluded from the study that heavy male viewers always feel less inclined to obey their parents yet still prefer the Korean family system. They endorse non-traditional Korean norms such as questioning one's parents and were significantly less likely to uphold the traditional value of filial piety. Thus greater AFKN viewing for males goes with apparent conflict between having more hostile views towards Westernisation, yet embracing some of its manifestations.

Kuo-Yi Wu (1990) studies the role and contribution of TV in the shaping of social perceptions such as sex roles, crime and violence, inter-personal relationships and ageing in Taiwan. In terms of perception of sex roles, contribution of TV viewing is distinctly contingent upon the background and other social conditions. A more liberal stance is related to heavy viewers of either Chinese or American programmes among females and those with high parental education. They generally prefer the foreign programme to the indigenous programmes. A consistent and significant relationship is found between weekday viewing and a more mistrustful worldview.

The study by Kang (1989), a pioneering work in Asia, measures the pervasiveness of the cultural outlook in Korean TV programming. The study focused on Korean students' perceptions about traditional and Western values in terms of sex roles, the family system, violence and social deviance. He conducted his study on 1,169 Junior High School students in Seoul, Korea. Although the findings are not statistically enormous, they seem to indicate that the heavy Korean TV viewing is weakly related to traditional sex-roles, to liberal attitudes towards dating and marriage, and to a distorted social reality on violence and social dominance. Kang then went on to detail the drastic influence of foreign TV programmes on sex-roles. Korean students who watch more AFKN are more likely to take more liberal positions on the sex-role attitudes. He apprehended that, compared to males, females are predisposed to think and behave in certain non-traditional ways such as wearing jeans and willingness to discount Confucianism. The females also felt that they would share dating expenses.

Karthigesu (1991) found undesirable behaviours in American programmes shown on Malaysian television. Boys and girls mix freely: are obsessed with having dates, parents encourage their daughter to date: watch approvingly amorous exchanges between daughter and her boyfriend, teenage school children kiss each other and talk about seduction and sex openly, adults kiss and make sexual overtures to each other in front of their children and children fix up dates for parents.

Phekoo *et al.* (1996) examined possible cultural consequences of US television programmes on 418 Trinidian students in the Caribbean island nation of Trinidad. The regions' lack of a domestic infrastructure to support indigenous television production combined with the close proximity to and shared language with the culturally influential United States has resulted in an overwhelming relevance on USA programming. The finding indicated that US TV was associated with liberal social values dealing with relationships family and authority. Liberal social values were defined in terms of behaving and thinking in social relations. The topic includes values dealing with dating and appropriate behaviours for school. Dating involves having a sexual relationship with one's partner, students should be free to hold hands during school hours, students should be free to embrace and kiss during school hours, children should have the same rights as parents and teachers and children should be allowed to dress as they wish for school. However, cultural knowledge and estimations of American's material wealth were not significantly associated with TV viewing.

Media researchers often express fears that youth who consume foreign media content are confused with the values projected in foreign programmes and the ones prevailing in the society. They generally prefer the foreign programmes to indigenous programmes. These findings support the contentions of cultural critics who assert that imported media into developing societies may undermine traditional values and cross cultural disruptions.

Action, adventure series, cartoons and films are the most prominent US produced programmes in broadcast schedules throughout Latin America. This enables comparisons between cable viewers and other TV viewers. A survey (Straubhaar and Gloria, 1991) on 15-year-old residents belonging to upper class in Santo Doming revealed that upper class respondents named the United States as a source of favourite programme far more often than lower class respondents (69% *vs.* 30%). Specifically upper class respondents frequently watch films in English, cartoons and foreign news significantly more often than middle class and lower class respondents. The study found social class was significantly related to a preference for US programmes. Education is also related to the preference for a particular programme. University educated viewers watch more US genres and fewer Dominican genres. Sex is also significantly related to preferring viewing programmes of particular origin. Women more than men mentioned Dominican Republic as a source of favourite programme. This finding reinforces the key idea in much of the cultural dependency literature that these classes will become culturally oriented towards the US as a dominant economic, political and cultural power in the region.

The application of satellite TV distribution system in Canadian Arctic native communities has led to a new form of electronic colonialism. After Eskimos were exposed to two and a half year's regular Canadian Broadcasting Corporation programmes, the research results demonstrated significantly a significant shift towards Euro Canadian Culture (Coldevin, 1979). He maintains that the cultural replacement gap between adults and adolescents will increase with sustained exposure to southern TV. Adults tended to be more attached to traditional norms than the adolescents. One of the most visible spin-off effects of TV as a window on the world function is assumed to be an expansion of viewers' preferred travel horizons.

TV was introduced in American Samoa in 1964. But by 1978-79, programmes of 14 hours per week were of local origin compared with imported programmes of 174 hours per week. A study conducted in 1972 on cultural values was replicated after 5 years and it was found that the teenagers have become more westernised in that period (Thomas, 1994).

The field studies have typically found that the content of the nation's TV can both increase awareness and marginally increase favourable perceptions of individual viewers towards the sender nation. A Venezuelan study found that liking the US was positively related to exposure to TV entertainment series, foreign news via newspapers and knowledge about the USA (McNelly and Fausto, 1986). Skinner (1984) found that those who watched more US programmes had a more positive image of the US and a less favourable image of Trinidad. Tsai (1970) in a study among Taiwanese children who watch TV found that they favoured elements of American culture and have a less favourable attitude towards their own culture than their non-viewing counterparts. In the related study she found that the interests of Chinese children had expanded after two years of watching the American programmes.

But, Babi (1990) in Cameroon concluded that youth would have a favourable attitude towards elements of foreign culture and a strong preference for locally produced programmes. The youth experienced the influence of TV on the way they dress. His study supports the theory that the TV's impact would be pervasive in some aspects as well as stimulates changes in others. But Payne and Peake (1977) in their study on viewers in Iceland found that the USA TV was only minimally effective in generating favourable attitude about USA or in creating attitudes of fear, anger or sadness which Icelanders commonly associated with USA culture. These studies tell us that culture promoted by the media coexist in popular life with existing norms and structure of the family. Moreover, the influence of television messages depends not only upon skilful techniques of persuasion but also on family situation of the receipt ingrained attitudes and selective perceptions of various groups.

There has been a slight influx of state run Soviet TV appearing on American cable TV. Three experiments were conducted on USA viewers to see the change in the image of the Soviet Union (Lavin, 1991). The results of all the three studies indicated that the subjects who watched two sessions of indigenous Soviet TV formulated a significantly more positive opinion of the Soviet Union than the subjects who did not see the programmes. The interesting finding here is that viewers incorporate affective qualities from Televised images and generalise these evaluations to the nation that those images depict.

The case of Australian TV channels received in Papua New Guinea is another example of cultural imperialism. Due to the geographical location, Papua New Guinea falls into the footprints of different satellites and it has been able to receive TV signals from Australia in addition to signals from American TV. Sinebare (1997) analyses the programmes advertised by Austrian Broadcasting Commission TV (ABCTV) to see which culture was being promoted for each and every individual programme and how relevant these programmes were to Papua New Guinea. Are the explicit or implicit sex-related scenes acceptable in Papua New Guinea culture? He expressed concern over the volume of information being received but not intended for the Papua New Guinea's audience. An average of 23 hours of TV time daily has been transmitted with only about 16 per cent of the time of the programmes may be of some use to Papua New Guinea audience which is seriously affecting them socially and culturally in irreversible ways. He concludes that majority who live in urban area are virtually inundated with information, which is culturally irrelevant to Papua New Guinea audience. The expectations promoted on TV are beyond their economic means and the values and lifestyles portrayed contradict and conflict with those of their own culture. He does suggest that there is a new class of people gradually being homogenised in Papua New Guinea who are mentally Anglo-American or Australian and ethnically Papua New Guinean.

Ware and Michael (1994) analysed 17 quantitative studies from 16 publications using the meta-analysis approach. A significant positive association between exposure to entertainment programmes and the dependent variables suggest that programmes imported from US have a small but statistically significant impact on the foreign audience. The study revealed that exposure to US entertainment programmes is more likely to increase preference for American products and influence attitudes towards America. The study also says that exposure to US television programming alone will not automatically generate an adoption of US values. This impact is influenced by both study characteristics and types of dependent measure.

Elasmar and John (1997) conducted a meta-analysis on impact of foreign television on domestic audiences. The study includes 27 studies from 21 different countries. The meta-analysis revealed weak positive correlation between exposure to foreign television and viewer's knowledge, attitudes, beliefs, values and behaviour. There is no statistically significant relationship between exposure to foreign TV and the likelihood that audience members will hold positive attitudes towards the country originating the foreign messages. Exposure to foreign television increases the purchase of foreign products, especially clothing and other consumer products though the size of the increase is small because foreign television accounts for only 5 per cent of the variation in foreign product purchasing. But exposure to foreign television increases audience knowledge about the country originating the messages.

Social stereotypes comprise a special category of social reality that can be learned from TV. Recent studies have shown that characterisation of Americans by foreign audience corresponding to their prortrayal in TV programmes is closely related to the frequency of viewing American TV. For example, more than 80 per cent of the American programmes are dubbed in Thai language. A survey among the college and university students in Thailand indicated that Americans were characterized by the respondents as pleasure loving, athletic, individualistic, efficient, scientifically minded, artistic, intelligent and materialistic (Tan and Kultide, 1988). It was also found in another study that frequency of viewing "Dallas" and "Dynasty" in Taiwan and Mexico was related to stereotyping of Americans as aggressive, cruel, dishonest and pleasure loving (Tan, *et al,* 1986). The heavy viewers of American programmes emphasise the following terminal values listed in order of frequency: pleasure or exciting life, freedom, happiness, true friendship and mature love. The values least emphasised by the panel were: salvation, inner harmony, self-respect and world at peace. It is clear from the analysis that TV is the major source of social stereotyping of American among Thai and Mexican sample.

US programmes which portray images of American lifestyles predisposes foreign audiences favourably towards US cultural and economic standards and away from their native cultures as well as alter their perceptions towards America and American. In the Philippines the frequent viewing of American TV programmes among High School students led to an emphasis on non-traditional values such as pleasure rather than the traditional values such as salvation, forgiveness and wisdom (Tan *et al.*, 1987).

Foreign Television and Indian Experience

In India, the concept of Foreign Television Programmes (FTPs) is relatively a new phenomenon and worries over the effects of these programmes on indigenous culture have also been expressed. There have also been concerns about social stereotypes and culturally inappropriate programming.

Dyal (1992) who studied the reactions to the MTV channel in India found that a very large per cent of people thought that there would be no effect on music industry but felt that most of our musicians/

singers are copying the Western style of composing and singing. The respondents felt that younger generations of singers are getting close to Western culture and ignoring native culture. Fears were expressed over the other programmes on STAR TV: the younger generations would adopt the Western lifestyle; they would copy the Western ways of speaking and dressing, the children would be more inclined to Westernisation, with its glamour and emphasis on sex. Another complaint was that serials glorify Western values. There was, however, a positive note also: younger generations are likely to become smarter and more aware of everything they ought to know. In another study Rahim (1994) found that three out of five viewers said that programmes shown on STAR TV and BBC were more on keeping with present day Indian values and culture.

A survey (Goonasekera, 1995) of 263 viewers in two metropolitan cities revealed that the most popular channels were DD, STAR plus, BBC, Zee and Sun TV. Overall opinion towards foreign programme was positive. The elements not liked in foreign programmes were sex, vulgarity, violence and crime. But the overall opinion of the viewers was firmly against banning foreign television programmes.

Rao and Melkote (1998) found that audiences in Bangalore watched Western series less frequently than they did any other type of programme such as news, sports or music programmes. Rao (1999) conducted another study in and around Bangalore and found that over 60 per cent of the urban viewers and 97.5 per cent of the rural viewers did not watch Western programmes which limits the extent of its influence. There was an overwhelming agreement among both urban and rural groups that the cultural values of Indian programmes rather than Western programmes are more relevant in India.

Hagiwara, *et al* (1999) attempted to ascertain whether the values, attitudes and styles of behaviour imparted by global television were at variance with the values and outlook of the countries receiving such programmes. The research methodology included a content analysis of global as well as local programmes and a survey. However, content analysis of selected local and foreign television programmes were conducted only in India, Malaysia and Philippines because, as the results later showed, few people watched global television in Hong Kong and Japan, especially during prime time. Content analysis results reveal some negative values in foreign programmes such as unhealthy competition, greed, extra/premarital sex, rude manners, skimpy clothing on women and individualism were found. Some positive values such as courage, respect for authority, family togetherness and concern for others were also appeared. In local programmes, the most noticeable positive values were family solidarity, respect for elders, courage, concern for others and modesty. As regards the negative values of the local programmes, greed, extramarital affairs, women behaving improperly (such as drinking and smoking) and manipulation were the major undesirables.

The thesis of media/cultural imperialism stipulates that the values portrayed in global television have a deleterious effect on local cultures. The audiences of the five societies were therefore asked if they believed that global television had a negative impact on themselves or their cultures. It was found out that more than half of the respondents in all the societies under study, except Japan, considered Western or US programmes to be more sexually explicit than local programmes. Japan also had a little more than one-third (38%) of respondents who held such a view. In other words, the Asian audiences did perceive some negative values such as sex and violence in global television. However, when they were asked if Western programmes corrupted their cultures, just about one-third or less than one-third of respondents in India (22%), Malaysia (37%) and the Philippines (34%) said 'yes'. The majority of respondents answered 'no' or 'neutral'. When the respondents were further asked whether Western programmes adversely affected their way of living, even less confirmation was found. The above findings show that only a minority of Asian audiences perceived any negative impact on their cultures, way of living, children, and local television production. On the other hand, more Asian audiences valued the benefits of global television. One-third (34%) of Indian, 41 per cent of Malaysian, and 72 per cent of Hong Kong respondents considered that global television could enrich their culture. Across all the five societies, more than two-thirds of respondents agreed that global television can help them understand other cultures, and over 80 per cent agreed that it could enrich their knowledge.

Though, there is some evidence that Foreign Television Programmes influence its viewer, a very little research is gathered to examine the socialisation process of FTP on different audiences.

In sifting the literature on the subject, one finds that the programmes as well as the viewers have been approached in different ways, reflecting different conceptualisations about foreign TV programmes. The existensive research done by researchers around the globe has opened up a number of important areas of inquiry for future studies. The results also suggest that social theorists, psychologists and economists working in other areas can adopt a more dynamic and conceptual approach to the analysis of FTP. The researcher could select the variables for the present study, after reviewing this massive literature.

The present study tries to address specific issues like change in family norms, attitudes towards roles of Indian women, sexual norms, lifestyles and music preferences. Does Foreign TV alter the attitudes of youth? The new media environment ushered in by FTP provides a context for examining these issues. Moreover India with cultural diversities, religious pluralism, multiplicity of languages and educational and economic disparities which is so different from the western nations made communication the most challenging task in contemporary India. The study tries to document the FTP influence on attitudes of Indian youth.

3

Values in the East and West

Culture is the way of life in a specific society. Every culture has its own value system. Culture in socialisation tells people what to do and what not to do. But there is no uniform definition of culture. "Culture is the sum of the available descriptions through which societies make sense of and reflect their common experience". (Williams, 1977: 35) Williams states "culture is a way of life". Explaining William's definition of culture, Hall (1986: 36) interprets that "culture is not a practice nor is it simply the descriptive sum of the mores and folkways of societies—as it tended to become in certain kinds of anthropology. It is threaded through all social practices and is the sum of their inter-relationships".

The international working group on training of personnel engaged in the production and dissemination of cultural goods and services, co-sponsored by UNESCO (1986) states that culture is not to be interpreted in the restricted sense of art alone. It encompasses the whole gamut of phenomena ranging from sports to educational programmes, from the motivation of creative artists to the habituation of the audiences, from the simple consumption of cultural products to self-generated cultural activities.

Culture is conceptualized in a variety of ways and now widely used in inter-cultural communication. Although culture is defined in terms of a nation—state, most people conceptualise culture in terms of race, social class and gender identity etc.

Cultural patterns are normative to the extent that they represent the fundamental values and practices accepted by the whole society. The way television is now integrated into family activities, television will be influenced by and will reflect the broader socio-cultural norms of the society, and add new dimensions to the existing values. "Value is a term used to refer to basic principle that we live by—our sense of what we ought and ought not do in our relations with the environment and the people in it" (Ruben, 1984:177). Values form the basis of most human behaviours. They are deep-rooted, hidden somewhere beneath the whole complex of peoples' value systems. Value is the cultural inheritance of the people. It is transmitted from generation to generation and it guides the actions of the people.

There are certain differences between Western social norms and norms guiding Indian society. Norms are rules for behaving. A norm is an abstract pattern that sets certain limits on behaviour. These differences are particularly noticeable in areas such as marriage as an institution, gendering of roles in the family, sexuality, generational disparity and so on. The Western process of selecting marriage partner is based upon love and self-choice. In the West, personal happiness and affection of the partners for each other are predominant factors leading to marriage. In India, couples seeking marriage rely upon their parents, relatives, friends and acquaintances. Thus arranged marriage is the norm in India. Marriage, for the male and the female is considered to be absolutely necessary by a majority among the Indians, which may not be the case in the West.

With regard to the participation of women in the family affairs, Western women's typical control over family finance is an expression of exercising her individual freedom. A wide range of British and American studies point to the emergence of highly home-centred way of life. These studies suggest that rising living standards are associated with an increasing investment of resources, time and energy in the home and in family leisure. They provide evidence of the growing involvement of men in the daily routines of family life and egalitarianism between husband and wife and parents and children and point to the construction of the nuclear family as a primary source of personal happiness and self-fulfilment (Elliot, 1996a). In India too, women are changing from being dependent on husband/father, to becoming bread-earners. This is especially the case with urban women. The spread of education and the changing nature of the job market has opened up many new jobs. More and more women consider that taking up a job helps in developing self-respect and self-identity. In the Indian society, traditional and hierarchical perceptions and functions of women are slowly giving way to more democratic ones. Despite these improvements in the status of women, traditional roles of women in the family have not completely changed.

There is a widely shared belief that in many Western societies today, there is more estrangement and lack of continuity between generations than in the early decades of the 20th century. The apathy of parents and lack of parental authority are cited as reasons partly responsible for the premarital pregnancy in the USA (Feldman and Margaret, 1985). An increasing proportion of single adults live alone in the Western societies. The proportion of families with children under 18 headed by lone parent was 24 per cent in 1990 (Statistical Abstract of the United States, 1992). The United States, in particular has played host to a spectacular growth of gay sub-culture (Elliot, 1996b: 18).

The major historical change in family values has been the one from a collective view of the family to one of individualisational sentiment. Over the past several decades, American families have been experiencing an increasing emphasis on individual priorities and preferences over collective family needs. The individualisation of family relations has also led to an exaggerated emphasis on emotional nurture, intimacy and privacy as the major base of family relations. It has contributed for the erosion of resistance of the family and its ability to withstand crises. Moreover it has contributed to a greater separation among family members especially to isolation of the older people (Hareven, 1988).

The family system is in a state of transition in India. The Indian society shows a marked tendency for the old cultural patterns and the new ethos to co-exist. Strong traces of the traditions can be seen in the modern families. Numerous survey results have shown that in many families, members may accept to some extent the authority of the oldest male though they no longer live with them (Goode, 1987). In India in general, children, especially, sons are considered as assets because they are supposed to provide care for the elders. Due to the urbanisation and modernisation and the emergence of the two-worker units, Indian families are witnessing some changes. Large families have devolved into nuclear units. A much higher rate of both divorces and remarriages are found. Also, the number of single parent families is increasing and a dramatic liberalization of sexual norms and practices has been taking place in India.

There are differences on issues of sexual morality between Indian and Western societies. Williams (1997) discovered that students in the United States are most likely to select romantic relationship as the closest relationship. In the USA dating pattern that emerged in the twenties provided youth the opportunity to engage in premarital relationship and their incidence began to increase in late 1960s and 1970s (Henslin, 1985:213). Parents assume a greater role in arranging dates. Increasingly, younger generation became sexually interested which led to sexually active college dormitory life and the explosive increase in the number of couples living together without being married (Feldman and Margaret, 1985). Sexual intercourse seems to have become an integral part of unmarried heterosexual relationships. More significantly, acceptance of unmarried sexual relationships seem to have evolved into acceptance of unmarried cohabitation. In the USA, researchers have also documented near universal participation in unmarried sex and increasing rates of partnership-turnover. (Wellings *et al.* 1994). Review of current research suggests that one quarter to one-half of married women have at least one extra-marital relationship after marriage and that about 50 to 65 per cent of the married men stray before the age of 40 (Lawson, 1988: 75). Another trend is towards casual relationships among youngsters.

In the Indian situation, for many years, the sex act was considered a secret. Even today majority of Indians including even married couples do not discuss sex openly. In general, Indians can be said to have conservative attitude in comparison with their more liberal Western counterparts. Dating is a relatively recent phenomenon. Today in India there is a growing tendency towards permissiveness and the relaxation of norms governing sexual behaviour. Despite these changes, the Indian family is much more stable than its counterparts in the West at the social level (Beteille, 1999).

There is a popular belief in the USA that the state of family has declined and that such decline is in some way tied to decay in the way in which families are portrayed on American Television. Many of these serials are now available to audiences across the world. It is imperative to understand the family relations in the foreign television programmes to measure its effects. Comstock and Strzyzewski (1990) for example analysed family interactions in prime-time TV programmes and noted that both parent-child, and sibling relations were defined by high levels of conflict and widely mutual blaming and providing negative criticism. Frequent absence of mother and daughter relationship is observed in soap operas (Liebes and Livingstone, 1992). Instead of bringing up their own daughters, mothers abandon them in an uncaring and sometimes cruel manner. Douglas and Olson (1996) examined TV portrayals during the period 1954-1992. They observed that in the families shown on TV husband-wife relationship were more expressive and hence appeared, on one hand, more overtly affectionate and, on the other, conflictual.

Majority of people believe that parent's willingness to discipline children in the families on television has diminished in the last decade (Marks, 1996) and the children now care for their parents less than in the past (Mellman, 1990; Kost, 1996). Family relations have become more conflictual so that members of modern families are more likely to ignore, evade and withdraw from each other (Akins, 1986, Comstock & Strzyzewski, 1990 and Heintz, 1992). Some researchers have reported that in the parent-child relations on TV children typically conform to parental authority (Skill *et al.* 1990) and parents tend to command and provide reassurance.

These studies on American Television Programmes indicate the possible effects on young viewers. Now with the availability of direct broadcast satellite technology, these American programmes are available to audiences worldwide exposing the youth to a different kind of family relations. But very little research evidence is available on how these programmes contribute to the changes in family life in other countries.

Television and Gender

There is some evidence that women viewers react to the media messages quite differently from male viewers. Hence it is imperative to examine how men and women interpret the television messages.

Youth binds both boys and girls in common ideology of life but gender guides them towards separate spheres of cultural experience. Gender role socialisation is a complex process involving an individual's family experience, cultural conditioning and education (Thornes, 1986). The gender socialisation not only shapes how individuals assess and create social reality cognitively, but also superimposes male-female differences on virtually every aspect of human experience, from modes of dress and social roles to ways of expressing emotion and sexual desire (Bem, 1993).

Communication researchers became interested in representation of woman in popular culture during the 1970s. In fact many of the researchers were feminists themselves, who were interested in studying the problem because of their own concern about a woman's place in society. In particular, feminist researchers were concerned about children's attitudes towards women, namely women should be dependent and that they have limited choices about their lives. Feminist scholars argue that inquiry in intercultural communication must address interlocking and overlapping nodes of identity, race, class and gender rather than focus on any one node alone.

Early studies show some evidence to support the argument that women react to media contents differently. For example in the UK women tend to watch 10 per cent more TV on an average than do men (Goodhardt *et al.* 1987: 8). In Denmark on the other hand girls tend to watch less video than boys and go less often to the cinema (Tufle, 1986). Husbands in lower class British homes dominate the remote control and wives talk on the telephone to cultivate social networks and intimacy (Silverstone *et al.* 1989). Modleski (1982) saw compatibility with women's style of housework in the repetitive, segmented rhythm of soap opera 'loving with a vengeance'. Hobson (1982) who studied the British popular soap opera 'Crossroads' found that women viewers were interested in resolutions of problems shared by women in networks with male peers, building a familial support system and preparing themselves for risk-taking in future work endeavours. In his study of the place of TV viewing in family, Morley (1986) found gender difference in viewing preferences and styles. As Morley remarks, it is the male who makes the viewing decisions when a conflict arises at home about what to watch on TV. Cultural feminists argue that women are culturally different from men and that women's culture should be treated as analytically distinct to that of men.

It can be unequivocally said that even today gender in India is one of the most important factors in social stratification. The norms and values regarding social behaviour of women are certainly more inflexibly codified and maintained in comparison to men. Deeply embedded cultural values and beliefs about the division of labour between men and women, marriage norms, different sex codes, and leisure activities may also influence the male perception of women.

From birth, one is socialised into a gender role according to the norms of one's culture. With restrictions on marriage, behaviour, leisure activities, participation of women in fine arts and differential sexual codes in India, it was assumed that the perceptions of women about FTP might vary from those of men. The media habits of people and their impact on the perceptions are likely to reflect pre-existing differences in status, power and values (Hornig *et al.* 1993).

Keeping these factors in mind, five socio-cultural variables have been identified for the study; family norms, social roles of Indian women, lifestyle, sexual norms and music preferences. It was also hypothesized that men react more positively to the Western family norms, sex norms, lifestyles and music in the programmes than do women. But with the rising urge in women for self-identity, women rather than men may show greater acceptance of the Western social roles of women. Thus in this study gender factor is also considered in examining the impact of FTP.

4

Paradigm and Plan of Study

Since 1991, India has experienced a sudden growth of cable television with the entry of a number of Foreign and Indian private satellite channels. As a result, Indians have now access to a variety of programmes, including Foreign Television Programmes (FTP). In a short time FTP have become very popular especially among the urban young audiences.

Further, television viewing is no more restricted to upper middle class and upper class segments of the Indian society as earlier. With the television sets being differentially priced, each family is bound to find some television set appropriate to its economic means. So it has become a common household item across all sections including the middle and lower classes. With the popularity of FTP, fears have been expressed that indigenous cultural values may be affected and eventually displaced and foreign values and lifestyles may take their place. As Schiller (1976) puts it, importing programmes is importing lifestyles and exposure to FTP may transform the values of the youth. Schiller defines cultural imperialism as a process of imposition of cultural institutions and values on the less developed nations or dependent states by the developed countries. There is a general sense of concern about these programmes and their impact on the young audience particularly if they are heavy viewers of FTP. Most of the FTP are telecast in English language which only a limited percentage of the audience in India can understand. But reports indicate that serials and musical programmes on these foreign channels are quite popular among the young people despite the language barrier (Dyal, 1992). One has to accept that these FTP provide a stiff competition to the Indian Broadcasting and have become a part and parcel of urban audience's choices.

While the popularity of the FTP persists, so do fears that these programmes are detrimental to the values of Indian masses. The cultural expressions in FTP in terms of behavioural norms and values and lifestyles are seen to be different from those prevailing in Indian society. But little attention has been paid to actual consumption of these programmes and their impact on the varied audiences. It has been recognised that effects of FTP are not uniform on all people. The research is yet to produce substantial data on the effects of FTP on Indian viewers. The research in this direction in India is very sparse. What needs to be studied is whether exposure to FTP influences the attitudes of youth. Does a young person's attitude reflect the values, which he or she sees on FTP?

This study makes an attempt to collect reliable data on effects of FTP on young minds. In addition, the study aims at developing a better understanding of the influence of FTP and their role in changing attitudes of the younger generation. An understanding of effects and influence of FTP on attitudes of young people is likely to help the policy-makers to take appropriate measures. Before proceeding further one needs to understand the theoretical framework and plan of study.

Theoretical Framework of the Study

The framework of this study is based on the Social Learning theory. According to Albert Bandura, Social Learning theory approaches the explanation of human behaviour in terms of a "continuous reciprocal interaction between cognitive, behavioural and environmental determinants" (Bandura, 1977: vii). The other principal understanding of Social Learning theory is tied up to the social context of learning. Bandura has emphasised the fact that people who observe responses of individuals tend to exhibit the same responses when placed in similar settings.

According to Bandura, behaviours and responses that are repeated, perceived as real, distinct, functional and salient are more likely to be attended to, thus more likely to be learned. When observing an event, which receives some kind of reward like social approval, pleasant experience and when the observer feels confident to perform, its symbolic imitation is facilitated. The social cognitive principle has been widely employed to explain the TV effects on a variety of social issues such as aggression, ethnic stereotypes and alcohol attitudes and behaviour. It also stresses the importance of viewer's cognitive activities when consuming TV messages (Bandura, 1977).

Any person's socialisation process is influenced by innumerable factors such as family, school, environmental factors etc. Direct experience and participation are important parameters which shape the youth's impressions of the perceived structure of their environment. However these forms of experience are usually limited to the immediate environment. The mass media, particularly the television, play a crucial role in bringing the outside world into homes. The mass media as an important institution enters the socialisation process of an individual

The Social Learning theory explains how environment influences the behaviour of an individual. Despite the general nature, "Social Learning theory is particularly relevant to study the impact of mass communication because the description and portrayal of social life is a frequent subject in media content" (DeFleur and Sandra, 1989: 216).

The actions of the characters in the audio-visual media can serve as a model for others to imitate. Modelling theory is also useful for describing the application of the general Social Learning theory which explains how new behaviours are acquired by people from media portrayals. An individual observes a character, identifies him/her as a model and remembers the actions of the model and performs them when confronted with similar circumstances (DeFleur and Sandra, 1989). Literature has shown that both children and adolescents acquire attitudes, emotional responses and new styles of conduct from the media espccially from films and television (Bandura, 1973 and Liebert *et al.* 1973). The theory clearly establishes that the media can serve as agents in the socialisation process.

Based on the Social Learning theory, the present study hypothesizes that the characters and their behaviour in FTP serve as models for heavy viewers of FTP. The viewers of FTP may acquire certain characteristics, which in turn influence their attitudes. It is also assumed that the younger generation is vulnerable to influences and tends to be inclined towards change. The younger people would serve as barometer to assess the influence of these FTP. Hence young students were selected for the study to determine the degree to which their attitudes were influenced by FTP.

Now with the availability of the foreign programmes, an important question arises: Does a young person's behaviour reflect what he/she has seen on the screen? The impact of foreign TV programmes on young people involves a number of indispensable factors such as interest in the programmes, viewing patterns, attitude towards the programmes and models of social reality that they promote.

The study aims at finding out whether and to what extent Foreign Television Programmes influence the attitudes of youth. The researcher aimed at finding answers to questions such as what the youth think about these programmes in terms of their preference and relevance, whether they experience an impact of these programmes on their attitudes or not.

Plan of Study

Objectives

The study focuses on the youth's television viewing activity at home in the environment of their families where they are normally exposed to television. The study intends to find out whether viewing of foreign television programmes influences the socio-cultural attitudes of the youth. The following are identified as objectives of the study:

- To find out the relation between viewing of foreign television programmes and acceptance of Western family norms,
- To find out the relation between viewing of foreign television programmes and acceptance of Western social roles for Indian women,
- To find out the relation between viewing of foreign television programmes and acceptance of Western lifestyles,
- To find out the relation between viewing of foreign television programmes and acceptance of Western sexual norms, and
- To find out the relation between viewing of foreign television programmes and preference for Western music.

In addition to these objectives, an attempt was also made to find out (i) the respondents' channel preferences, (ii) their programme preferences on foreign television channels, (iii) who decides what programmes to be watched in the family, (iv) discussions on foreign television programmes, (v) impact of watching foreign television programmes on the viewing of Indian channels, and (vi) the bearing of parental background such as education, occupation and income on the viewing levels of the respondents.

Hypotheses

1. Young heavy viewers of foreign television programmes tend to show a greater degree of acceptance of Western family norms than moderate and low viewers of foreign television programmes.
2. Because of heavy viewing of foreign television programmes, young male viewers tend to show a greater degree of acceptance of Western family norms than young female viewers.
3. Young heavy viewers of foreign television programmes tend to show a greater degree of acceptance of Western social roles for Indian women than moderate and low viewers of foreign television programmes.
4. Because of heavy viewing of foreign television programmes, young female viewers tend to show a greater degree of acceptance of Western social roles for Indian women than young male viewers.
5. Young heavy viewers of foreign television programmes tend to show a greater degree of acceptance of Western sexual norms than moderate and low viewers of foreign television programmes.
6. Because of heavy viewing of foreign television programmes, young male viewers tend to show a greater degree of acceptance of Western sexual norms than young female viewers.
7. Young heavy viewers of foreign television programmes tend to show a greater degree of acceptance of Western lifestyles than moderate and low viewers of foreign television programmes.
8. Because of heavy viewing of foreign television programmes, young male viewers tend to show a greater degree of acceptance of Western lifestyles than young female viewers.

9. Young heavy viewers of foreign television programmes tend to show a greater degree of preference for Western music than moderate and low viewers of foreign television programmes.
10. Because of heavy viewing of foreign television programmes, young male viewers tend to show a greater degree of preference for Western music than young female viewers.

Method of Research

"Survey" method is adopted which obtains the data from large, representative but diverse and widely scattered groups of the population, Surveys "are not simply restricted to the collection of information about things, and this makes them a useful method for finding out about the individual opinions, attitudes, behaviour and so on towards a whole range of topics and issues" (Hansen, 1998: 225). Survey researchers describe the characteristics of a set of cases and at the same time explain causes of phenomena. The "survey analysis tries to locate causes by comparing cases" (de Vaus, 1993: 5).

Survey researchers seek an understanding of what causes some phenomenon. However survey researchers need to be careful, to avoid mistaken attribution of causal links. The present study was conducted between December 1998 and January 1999.

Variables of the Study

The variables selected in the study, namely family norms, social roles of Indian women, sex norms, lifestyles and music preferences have been explained below in detail.

Family Norms

Family is the basic institution of any society and is primarily responsible for socialisation of the young. The value system in the Indian family has been undergoing changes due to industrialisation, urbanisation, modern education, modern medicine, legal system, family planning policies and media (Agrawal, 1995). Along with other factors mass media, especially Television contribute to an extent to the value system of the family. Television has taken over many of the traditional socialisation functions of the family.

At present the study of Television as an activity is of enormous importance to understand the intra-family relations across cultures. Families portrayed in TV programmes usually behave in ways that make sense to viewers and are treated by viewers as authentic (Lewis, 1991). As such, TV families seem to offer lessons about appropriate family life (Cantor and Cantor, 1992) and in a more general sense, affect the way in which people think about the family (Anderson, 1993). Goodman (1983) notes that psychologists often focused on the dining room table as a way to understand family functioning. She suggests, however, that given television's acknowledged pervasiveness in our lives, many families develop and negotiate rules or principles, governing areas of behaviour on the basis of what they view on TV. Family members discuss what they watch and come to a collective understanding about it, which is how the messages of the media enter into a culture (Katz and Liebes, 1984). Lull (1988) says that values implicit in programming are distributed through family and friendship networks to all of society. The satellite technology has given the opportunity to Indian viewers to peep into the Western families. The FTP with different family norms gives a chance to examine its impact on Indian viewers and how it affects their attitudes towards a family system. Hence the family norms are taken as a variable and changes in the attitudes towards family norms due to FTP are examined in the study.

Family norms refer to the standards of behaviour and rules of conduct expected by the members of the family in their relationships with the other members of the family. Such norms are generally implicit and informal and require no formal codification. They are transmitted from generation to generation through the process of socialisation within a given culture. They involve relationships such as husband-wife, parent-child and the elder-younger, codes concerning love, co-operation, respect, authority roles and so on. With the availability of foreign television programmes, the Western family structure, norms and relationships are said to be more familiar to the youth than before.

Thus the family norms are operationalised into 17 dependent variables. They include involvement of father, mother and young members of the family in the process of decision-making, children's relationship with their parents, financial dependence of children on their parents, respect for elders and opinions on love marriages, nuclear families, wedding rituals etc.

Social Roles of Indian Women

The spheres of men's and women's activities tend to be sharply separated in the Indian society. An Indian woman is expected to perform certain roles within the framework of the social structure. The role is a segment of culture. It consists of behavioural norms bearing a one-to-one correspondence with social structure.

Women in Indian families perform multiple roles such as keeping house, preparing food, taking-care of children and the aged. Men are expected to focus more on their jobs and on matters outside the family, while women are expected to be more nurturing, integrative and domestic. Goldberg (1994) states on the basis of ethnographic evidence that Indians regard women as inferior and dependent. However, even if a working woman is accepted as inevitable, traditional ideas still dominate even among the intellectuals (Kapadia,1995). Working women receive relatively little help from their families in making adjustment with regard to demand on their time and pressures of work. The welfare of the family is supposed to weigh more with women than their career. As each of the two roles as a homemaker and as a working woman makes demands on time and involves physical and mental participation, the women is continuously under stress in making adjustments and hence changes in her traditional roles of a wife and mother are inevitable. Education has brought women out of the confines of their homes and put them in contact with the philosophy of liberalism. This too has contributed to a modification of the relationship between husband and wife.

It is already evident that the portrayal of women in the mass media has a direct influence on the self image of the growing girl child who is likely to unconsciously emulate the ideal as projected by the media (Verma, *et al.* 1995:8). FTP show both husband and wife sharing the tasks of earning and homemaking. It would, therefore, be interesting to find out whether exposure to FTP has brought about a change in youth's perceptions of women's role in Indian society.

The dependent variable, social roles of Indian women, is operationalised in terms of 13 indicators which include opinions on decision-making, traditional division of labour between husband and wife such as sharing household chores, taking care of children, assertion of women of their own rights, economic independence, and opinions about married women going out to work and about an ideal Indian family.

Sexual Norms

As a component of social action sexual behaviour is also a way of expressing and conveying both individual and social meanings. Social norms can prescribe sex related roles. Norms are rules for behaving. Examination of sex norms in Western and Indian societies indicates a clear-cut disparity between the two cultures. In India, sex is a part of marriage; it is not allowed before and outside marriage. In general, strict adherence to this norm has been demanded of women while men are often allowed to get away with greater freedom with regard to this norm. By implication, separate moral codes for men and women seem to exist in Indian society.

For long, sex was regarded as a personal and private issue. But in recent years, with media liberalisation, there has been an invasion of privacy of the Indian households by the Western media. A large number of Western television programmes with a high degree of sexually explicit scenes and information are now freely available and suddenly sex seems to lose its old taboo. Moreover, there is evidence that the media do exercise some influence over the development of worldviews including values and norms with respect to gender and sexual orientation.

Thus it was decided that an attempt be made to correlate the amount of FTP viewing and change in attitudes towards sex norms. The dependent variable sex norms is operationalised into ten components. Opinions on whether exposure to FTP stimulates interest in sex, encourages the young to indulge in casual sex as well premarital, exta-marital and unnatural relationships (such as homosexualism and lesbianism) and opinions on Western pattern of dating are sought.

Lifestyles

Lifestyle is defined as the integration of decisions in the realms of career, personal and family relationship and leisure that result in guiding principles which direct one's life (Peterson, 1994: 513). Lifestyle also includes clothing, food, accent and leisure pursuits. A person's qualifications, educational experience, occupation and levels of responsibility within his/her culture also determine his/her lifestyle.

The youth are avid viewers of foreign television programmes in India (Dyal, 1992). It is assumed that viewing of foreign television programmes could influence the youth' choice of what they consume, how they behave, what they aspire to be and what they ultimately become.

The dependent variable lifestyle is opeationalised into ten components. The study makes an attempt to see how foreign television programmes influence the lifestyles such as food habits, hair styles, dress designs, and imitation of mannerisms, behavioural patterns, jargon, accent used by the character in FTP and looking up to them as role models.

Music Preferences

Music is an expression of inner life, an expression of feeling through the technique of composition, according to the rules of a certain music style. Music operates for specific purposes in all cultures and analysis of these processes reveals much about both specific and general behaviour. Song texts and social behaviour that accompanies music are an extremely important index to basic values. The audience responds to the music in physical and psychological ways. Research indicates that viewers can be affected by the content of the videos they watch. Viewers show increased liking for the behaviour they watch in music videos. Researchers have found that popular music plays an important role in adolescent sub-cultures and subsequent socialisation to the mainstream culture. Music videos and MTV in particular seeming to have carved out a permanent niche in the electronic psyche of teen and young adult audiences (Hansen, 1994). Despite disparities between Western and Indian music styles, music is the one cultural space, which seems to belong to the young people. Music fulfils the emotional needs of the youth. Viewing popular music videos is an important form of entertainment and communication for the youth. It helps them as diversion.

Music also comes under the impact of Western culture. Western music is already pervading the Indian society. The spread of schools to teach Western dance and the popularity of music channels can be cited as an indication. Music has already created an international sub-culture among the youth all over the world. Hence the study examines the opinions of the youth about Western and Indian music and if there is a shift in their comparative preferences for Western and Indian music.

The variable, music preferences is operationalised into nine items: whether youth consider western music as modern, think that learning is necessary as it gives recognition among peers, whether it encourages them to participate in discotheques, whether it helps them to dance in parties and results in losing interest in Indian music.

Terms Used in the Study

The major terms used in the study are defined below:

Foreign Channel

Any channel beamed via satellite and distributed via cable telecasting a majority of its programmes in English as well as programmes originally made in English and later dubbed or sub-titled in any Indian language.

Indian Channel

Any channel, which telecasts a majority of its programmes in an Indian language except English.

Foreign Television Programmes (FTP)

Any programme telecast on the foreign channels in English as well as programmes originally made in English and later either dubbed or sub-titled in any Indian language.

Level of Viewing

The number of hours devoted for viewing foreign television programmes per week.

Low Viewer

The respondent who watches foreign television programmes for up to fourteen hours per week.

Moderate Viewer

The respondent who watches foreign TV programmes for fifteen to twenty one-hours per week.

Heavy Viewer

The respondent who watches foreign TV programmes for more than twenty-one hours per week.

Attitudes

A mental disposition towards persons, aspects and events that guides their acceptance or rejection. For this study, respondents' agreement or disagreement for a single item in each dimension on a given scale is considered as an attitude.

Western Norms

The western norms have been conceptualised into having five dismensions; namely, family norms, social roles of women, sexual norms, lifestyle and music preferences. Each of these five dimensions are defined below.

Family Norms

The family norms are operationalised into 17 dependent variables which broadly deal with five parameters. Each parameter of family norm is explained below:

1. *Equality of mother and father:* Acceptance of mother's involvement in decision-making on par with father.
2. *Practice of consulting the young in issues pertaining to them:* Acceptance of the concept of consulting the young in matters pertaining to them.
3. *Financial independence of young children:* Acceptance of the practice of financially independence of young children.
4. *Absence of the concept of obligation on the part of the children towards their parents:* Lack of Willingness on

the part of young children to use polite language in conversing with parents, to obey elders and to take care of the parents.

5. *Marriage related issues:* Acceptance of self-choice marriages, rejection of marriage rituals, preference for nuclear family and acceptance of the concept of live-in couples.

Social Roles of Women

The dimension of social roles of women is operationalised into 13 dependent variables which broadly deal with 4 parameters. Each parameter is explained below:

1. *Acceptance of the idea of career for women:* Acceptance of an active career for women on par with men.
2. *Sharing of family responsibilities by husband and wife:* Acceptance of the responsibilities of nurturing children and sharing of income generating and other household chores equally by husband and wife.
3. *Rejection of stereotypical image of a career woman as irresponsible:* Rejecting the idea that working woman are bad housewives and cause strain in the family.
4. *Acceptance of financial independence for women:* Acceptance of the idea of financial independence for women and their assertiveness without being conscious of reactions of the society.

Lifestyles

The dimension of lifestyles is operationalised into 10 dependent variables. Acceptance with the view of imitating mannerisms, behaviour, dress designs, hairstyles, accent and jargon used by the characters in foreign television programmes.

Sexual Norms

The dimension of sexual norm is operationalised into 10 dependent variables which deal with 3 parameters. Each parameter is explained below:

1. *Pre/extra/unnatural relations:* Acceptance of pre/extramarital relations as well as homosexual and lesbian relations as normal.
2. *Identical sex code for men and women:* Acceptance of identical sex code for men and women.
3. *Dating:* Acceptance of idea of dating.

Music Preferences

The dimension of music preferences is operationalised into 9 dependent variables which broadly deal with 2 parameters. Each parameter is explained below:

1. *Learning western music:* Acceptance of the idea that learning western music helps to dance in parties and give recognition among the peer.
2. *Shift in music preferences from Indian music to western music:* Acceptance of the idea that western music leads to disinterest in Indian music.

A Profile of Youth

Youth is a social category, which emerges in connection with a particular way of life (McNeill, 1988: 145). Defining the age category of youth is a difficult task. Eisenstadt (1972: 20) defines 'the period of youth as the period of transition from childhood to full adult status in the society'. The youth is not yet fully acknowledged as an adult, a full member of the society. Rather, he or she is being prepared or is preparing for such adulthood.

This transitional period in life is particularly vulnerable and dynamic. It is an age group that accounts for a substantive majority of the population in most Third World countries. The United Nations Statistics on children and youth assigns any person between 15 and 24 years of age to the category of youth (Nair *et al.* 1989:20). Many participants in the UNESCO regional youth conferences agree that the definition of youth applies to all the young and define being young as extending to 30 or 35 years of age depending upon their national experience (UNESCO Report, 1981:19). Thus the definition of youth has become broader and more flexible than before. There is no fixed age category where the young can be placed as the definition of youth varies with each nation and culture.

The present study follows the concept of 'youth' given in the UN statistics quoted above and regard youth as any male or female in the age group of 15 to 24 years. As such the present study focuses on the final year graduate students whose average age is around 20.5 years.

Method of Sample Selection

In the first phase, it was decided to choose Hyderabad, the capital city of Andhra Pradesh as the field for the study. Hyderabad, the fifth largest city in India is cosmopolitan in nature. Though the researcher belongs to Tirupati, Hyderabad was chosen for the survey, because of its cosmopolitan nature. It consists of heterogeneous population like Arabs, Pathans, Muslims, Rohilas, Sikhs, Bawahiris, Christians besides the Hindu who include Rajputs, Marwaris, Gujaratis and Maharashtrians who speak different languages. 'Telugu' is the state language. The city is rich in media activity. It consists of AIR and DD stations, film city, headquarters of Siti cable and a number of newspapers and magazines. Hyderabad city has six lakhs cable connections. Because of its cosmopolitan nature and multiplicity of languages and because of the children having their education through English medium and their parents' financial status, the children tend to watch FTP.

In Hyderabad, Osmania University, which is one of the oldest universities in the country, was chosen for the survey. Many of the degree colleges located in the twin cities are affiliated to Osmania University. The university has been a pacesetter in imparting modern education in the state. There are 123 degree colleges, which are affiliated to Osmania University. The colleges located in Hyderabad area were taken for the study.

The third phase consisted of selection of the colleges for the study. As the size of the university is very large, it was not feasible to approach every member of the population and hence the required number of colleges were chosen randomly for the study. The number of colleges chosen was 12. The composition of the colleges includes seven co-educational colleges, four girls' colleges and one boys' college. The colleges drawn for the sample are heterogeneous in nature in terms of infrastructure, teaching staff, students strength and other teaching aids. The sample consists of colleges with students strength of 450 to 2,500.

The fourth phase of sampling involved, choosing the units of research, namely the primary target group of students. Only the students studying in the final year of their undergraduate degree course in each of the three streams, *i.e.* Arts (B.A.), Commerce (B. Com.) and Science (B.Sc.) were chosen for the study. The average age of the students thus selected was found to be 20.5 years. It was felt that at this age students are mature enough to express their views independently on sensitive issues such as family, marriage, gender roles and sex norms. Further, by the time they reach final year of undergraduate study, they had sufficient exposure to foreign television programmes, if such an exposure has an impact on them. In each college 39 students were chosen randomly. Care is taken to give equal representation to each stream. It was also ensured that male and female students get equal representation in the primary target group. Thus possibility of bias in picking up the units was eliminated by the use of probability method.

A brief note on the nature of the sample, which includes the region, *i.e.*, Hyderabad, Osmania University and the colleges under study is given below.

A Profile of Hyderabad

The formation of the State of Andhra Pradesh with the beautiful and historic city of Hyderabad as its capital in 1956 is an important landmark in the history. Hyderabad was originally founded by Sultan Mohammed Quli Qutub Shah, the 5th king of the Qutub Shahi dynasty in 1590 A.D., at Golkonda. The Asaf Jahi rulers shifted their capital from Aurangabad to Hyderabad in 1761. The seventh Asaf Jah, ruled the Hyderabad Dominions from 1911 to 1948 at the end of which the state was merged into the Indian Union. He can be considered the chief architect of modern Hyderabad. It became the capital of the state of Andhra Pradesh, when it was formed a linguistic state in 1956 with Telugu as the principal language. With Secunderabad, it forms a twin city which is the fifth largest city in India.

Hyderabad has a population of 5.2 million approximately and a growth rate of 9.5 per cent. Hyderabad spreads in the areas of 250 sq. kms. Hyderabad ranks 5th in population among major cities in India (including the 4 metros) and 2nd in decadal growth. The historic city of Hyderabad now is 400 years old and growing faster than ever before.

Hyderabad, the city of learning, is known in the academic circles. It has 8 universities, 28 national level apex research and training institutions. Andhra Pradesh Infrastructural and Industrial Corporation is setting up a world class info-city with a state-of-art infrastructural facilities placing Hyderabad as Hitech city of global standards (Hyderabad Shahar.com). It has 4 large and 9 medium size dailies in English, 8 main and 20 small size Newspapers in Telugu, 6 dailies in Hindi and 9 dailies in Urdu.

A Profile of Osmania University

Osmania University, named after its royal founder Sir Mir Osman Ali Khan, Nizam VII, was established in 1918. It was the first University in India to start an evening college in 1950. Facilities were made available for the study of Sanskrit, Marathi, Telugu and Kannada languages along with the Urdu which was the medium of instruction. It is the eighth oldest University in India, the third oldest in South India and the first in the erstwhile princely state of Hyderabad. Osmania University is a multi-faculty, multi-campus, semi-residential with 21 constituent and 474 affiliated colleges, 953 faculty members, 2,989 non-teaching employees and 2,10,023 students. The University offers various Diploma, Undergraduate, Postgraduate and research courses. The jurisdictional area of the university covers nearly 60,000 kilometres, which has a population of nearly 20 million.

In addition to these colleges, the university has set up a number of research and training centres and advanced centres of excellence in the emerging areas of human endeavour and social relevance. The Centre for Distance Education also offers certain courses through Distance Education for the benefit of those who cannot join regular colleges as full-time students.

Teaching and research activities are carried out in the university through its eleven faculties, viz. Arts, Business Management, Commerce, Education, Engineering, Informatics, Law, Oriental Languages, Science, Social Sciences and Technology.

Profile of Colleges under Study

Haindavi Degree College

Established in 1993, Haindavi Degree College is a self-financing co-educational institution. The college offers degree courses leading to

B.Com. (General), B.Com. (Computers), B.Sc. and BCA. All the above courses are conducted through English medium. It has student strength of 400 with teaching staff strength of 15. The college is well equipped with laboratories, a modern computer centre and teaching aids. Haindavi Degree College has a good library with a good number of standard reference books.

Badruka College of Commerce and Arts

Established in 1950, Badruka College of Commerce and Arts offers bachelor's degree courses leading to B.Com. (General), B.Com. (Vocational) with specialization in advertising and marketing and also B.Com. (Computers). It is a co-educational institution. It has been rated as the State's best college in commerce education and eighth at the national level, according to the survey carried out by a weekly "*India today*". It has 650 students and 20 teaching staff. It has a library with good collection of books, and has 20 computers. The college has teaching aids like TV and over-head projector.

Osmania University College for Women

Established in 1924, Osmania University College for Women offers courses like B.A., B.Sc., B.Com., and BCA. In addition, it offers postgraduate courses and certificate courses which are primarily vocational. The college offers thirty-five courses at the undergraduate level, and 16 courses at the post-graduate level. The college has now about 2,600 students and staff strength of 126. The college has good laboratories, computer centre and teaching aids like over-head projector, slide projector and TV. The college also has access to the Internet.

New Science College

Established in the year 1995, New Science College offers courses leading to B.Sc., B.Com. (General) and BCA courses. The BCA course is offered in co-education and B.Sc. and B.Com. degree courses are offered only for girls. It offers instruction through English medium. It has a strength of 158 students with 24 teaching staff. Being a small institute it has a moderate library and a laboratory.

Priyadarshini Degree College

Established in the year 1996, Priyadarshini Degree College offers courses leading to B.Sc. and B.Com. (General). It is a co-educational institute. It being a young private institute, it has strength of 135 students and teaching staff is 10. It has no TV but has a laboratory and computer lab. It has a few reference books.

Geetanjali Degree College for Women

Established in the year 1994, Geetanjali Degree College offers B.Sc., B.Com. (General) and B.Com. (Computers) and B.C.A. It also offers intermediate courses. It has a student strength of 380 with 20 teachers. It has a Computer lab, TV and overhead projector. The library subscribes to journals and newspapers regularly.

Shadhan Degree College for Boys

Established in 1989, Shadhan Degree College for Boys offers courses leading to B.Sc., with 15 combinations, B.A., with 3 combinations and B.Com. It is considered to be a very established college in terms of staff and infrastructural facilities. It has on its roll 1000 students and 60 teaching staff. It has a well-equipped laboratory and Computer centre. It also has teaching aids like TV, OHP etc.

Kranthi Degree College

Established in the year 1995, Kranthi Degree College offers courses leading to B.Com. (General and Computes) and B.Sc. with different combination. It is a co-educational institute. The total strength of students is 540 with 35 teaching staff. It is a private college. It has no teaching aids and TV. It has a computer lab.

Human Resource Development Degree College

Established in the year 1990, Human Resource Development Degree College is a co-educational institute. The college provides instruction not only in the regular courses of B.A., B.Com. and B.Sc. but also has introduced restructured course combinations of Maths, Science,

Statistics with the subject like Computer Science, Electronics, Microbiology and Biochemistry. The student strength is around 1200 and 45 members on the staff. The college was granted affiliation to start PG Diplomas in MISCA and Taxation, the classes of which were started in the year 1998. It has a well established laboratory, computer lab and library. It has teaching aids like television, OHP projector and slide projector.

Raja Bahadur Venkatrama Reddy Women's College

Established in the year 1954, Women's college offers courses leading to B.A., B.Sc., B.Com. with 25 combinations. Science and Arts faculties were started at the Intermediate level with English medium. The college was upgraded into a degree college in the year 1957. Telugu was introduced, as medium of instruction in the year 1969-70 in addition to English medium. To keep abreast of the times Commerce was started in 1971. Another milestone in the history of the college was the introduction of Postgraduate course in Economics and Telugu in the year 1984-85. Under autonomy, new combinations like Mathematics, Physics and Computer Science, Mathematics, Statistics and Computer Science, Journalism, M.L. (English) and Computer Science were started. The college began with a strength of 59 students and has now grown and developed into a Postgraduate institution offering a number of courses and providing education to about 2,300 women students with 110 staff members. It has sophisticated infrastructure and library with 30,000 books on variety of subjects. They also have a audio-visual centre.

Annie Besant Women's College

Established in the year 1991, Annie Besant Women's College offers various courses belong to Science, Commerce and Management streams with 11 combinations. The institute has computer labs having 40 computers for B.Sc., B.Com. (Computers) and B.C.A. students. The College has fully equipped laboratories. The college has a team of 31 lecturers and 528 students. The college library has nearly 1500 books. The college also offers hostel facilities. It has audio-visual aids.

Badruka College for Information Technology

Established in the year 1990, Badruka College for Information Technology offers courses leading to B.Sc. Computers, BCA, MCA, M.Sc., and PG Diploma in MISCA. It has 500 students and 35 staff members. It has a good laboratory with 100 computers and has Internet facility. The library has 4000 books, computer journals and magazines. It also has satellite based interactive networks for educational training (SINET) facilities.

About the Questionnaire

The questionnaire has evolved over several iterations. The researcher collected the relevant literature extensively and discussed the issues with sociologists, psychologists and subject experts. The most important source was brainstorming sessions with the students. These discussions greatly facilitated the researcher in preparing the questionnaire. Questions were presented in a definite order, proceeding from the general to the more specific issues. This order helped the respondents to organise their own thinking and respond logically and objectively.

The questionnaire is broadly divided into two parts which consists of 15 questions. Besides the researcher collected information on demographic factors of the respondents like gender, age, parents' education, occupation, income and respondents' medium of instruction at the school and college. The intention was to see whether education and economic status of the parents have a bearing on the viewing patterns of the respondents. The first part of the questionnaire contains 10 questions which seek information about the duration of having cable connection, reasons for watching FTP programme and channel preferences of FTP, programme selectors in the family, and programme related discussion. Questions were also asked to examine the effect of viewing these programmes on the viewing of Indian channels and on the general activities of the respondents.

The second part of the questionnaire consists of five major questions to test the formulated hypotheses. Each question consists of a number of items, which seek to find the relationship between exposure of FTP and the extent of acceptance of western norms. Question 11 contains 17 items, assessing the respondents' agreement and disagreement with western family norms. Question 12 consists of 13 items dealing with the agreement or disagreement with western social roles for Indian women. Question 13 consists of 10 items dealing with the acceptance or rejection of Western sex norms. Question 14 consists of 10 items pertaining to the acceptance or rejection of western lifestyles. Question 15 consists of 9 items pertaining to shift if any in music preferences.

The questionnaires are given to the students who have cable connections and are viewing Foreign Television Programmes.

Pilot Study

A pilot study was conducted to review the questionnaire in terms of its relevance of the study and to assess the language used, the difficulty and ambiguity of the questions. The preliminary format was distributed among 50 students in two colleges in Hyderabad, namely New Government Degree College, Khairatabad and Keshav Memorial Degree College, Narayanaguda which were not a part of the final study.

The detailed comments offered by the subjects in the pilot study helped to improve the questionnaire. In the questionnaire used for the pilot study the subjects asked to mention the favourite programmes in the order of preference. For the convenience of the tabulation, the respondents were asked to mark only the three most preferred programmes on foreign channels in the final questionnaire.

The respondents found some statements vague and could not respond properly. The statement like 'music channels promoting indigenous music' was dropped. The questionnaire used for pilot study consists of statements like "FTP gives information about sex" and "music on foreign channels contains obscene visuals", were found irrelevant because they deal with the contents of the programming but not the influence and hence were deleted.

Based on the opinions expressed in the pilot study, questions on travel aspirations, financial independence of the youth, dating, youth participation in discotheques were incorporated in the final questionnaire.

Thus, the lessons derived from the pilot study were used in drafting the final questionnaire by modifying or rejecting some items and adding some new ones.

Method of Data Collection

After choosing the colleges, authorities were contacted for permission to conduct the study in their institutions. Questionnaire was administered personally to groups of individual students in a classroom situation. This enabled the researcher to interact with the students and explain the purpose of the study to them. Thus rapport was established with the respondents. The meaning of some items was explained when doubts were raised but care was taken to see that the respondents do not get influenced by the researcher's comments. The questionnaire was given to 468 respondents. Of them 234 were male students and 234 female students. Out of 468 questionnaires collected, 26 questionnaires were not filled properly and hence were rejected. Thus the size of the final sample stands at 442 which includes 230 male respondents and 212 female respondents.

Method of Data Analysis

It is a challenge to make a sense out of massive amount of data and reduce the volume of information, identify significant patterns and evolve a strategy for communicating the findings of the analysis.

The data was analysed mainly in terms of comparison of "Heavy", "Moderate" and "Low" viewers on each dependent variable. Total TV viewing varies depending upon the demographic differences. It varies from nation to nation and culture to culture. For example, German households on an average watch six hours and twelve minutes of television per day (Darschin, 1997), whereas American households watch TV for an average of nearly seven hours a day (Neilson Media Research, 1995).

For this study, respondents were asked to indicate the total number of viewing hours of foreign programmes per day separately during weekdays and weekends, because the number of total viewing hours varies from weekdays to weekends. The total viewing hours of foreign television programmes over a week was calculated. The total viewing hours of FTP per week range from 7 to 42 hours. On the basis of the number of hours per week devoted for FTP, the respondents were categorised into three categories: Heavy, Moderate and Low. The data was analysed among the three groups. In making the comparisons in the category of heavy viewers responses of male and female viewers were analysed separately and compared. The major statistical tool used for analysis was MANOVA.

5

Viewing Patterns of Youth

This chapter focuses on economic and educational status of the respondents' parents and tries to trace its influence on the viewing of FTP. Some of the earlier studies indicate that socio-economic background has a bearing on media habits of children and youth. The Surgeons General report (1972) also concludes that those adults whose parent's occupation and educational levels placed them in the lower socio-economic strata spent more time on watching TV than those at the higher socio-economic levels. Therefore this study makes an attempt to understand whether educational and economic background affects the viewing patterns of student respondents or not.

In the study, the sample, containing 442 respondents has been classified on the basis of the number of hours of Foreign Television Programmes (FTP) viewed into three categories, namely heavy, moderate and low viewers. Further, the respondents have been classified by gender. The distribution of sample in terms of the number and percentage of cases according to each parameter has been worked out using Statistical Package for Social Sciences (SPSS) routine.

The data is presented according to gender, course of study, medium of instruction at school and college and parents' education, occupation, income and duration of having cable connection. Further it also discusses the relationship between these factors and level of viewing. Some of the parameters are shown diagramatically.

Table 5.1: Gender-wise Distribution of Sample

Gender	*Total*	
	No.	*%*
Male	230	52.04
Female	212	47.96
Total	442	100.00

There were 442 respondents included in the sample. Among them, male respondents numbered 230 (52.04%) and the female respondents were 212 (47.96%) (Table 5.1).

Table 5.2: Course-wise Distribution of Sample

(*N=442*)

Course	*Male*		*Female*		*Total*	
	No.	*%*	*No.*	*%*	*No.*	*%*
B.A.	77	52.03	71	47.97	148	100
B.Com.	77	52.38	70	47.62	147	100
B.Sc.	76	51.70	71	48.30	147	100

Table 5.2 indicates the distribution of the respondents according to their course of study. Out of the 442 respondents those who are undergoing the course of Arts were 148, those undergoing Commerce were 147 and the remaining 147 students had registered in the course of Science. The table also indicates the male and female students in each course. The number of male respondents was slightly higher than the female respondents in each of the three courses.

In the course of Arts, there were 77 male respondents (52.03%) and 71 female respondents (47.97%). In the course of Commerce, the male students numbered 77 (52.38%) and the number of female students was 70 (47.62%). In the course of Science, the number of male respondents was 76 (51.70%) and that of female respondents was 71 (48.30%).

Table 5.3: Distribution of Respondents by their level of Viewing

Heavy		*Moderate*		*Low*		*Total*	
No.	*%*	*No.*	*%*	*No.*	*%*	*No.*	*%*
138	31.22	138	31.22	166	37.56	442	100

Table 5.3 indicates the distribution of viewers according to their level of viewing. Among the 442 respondents, heavy viewers were 138 (31.22%), moderate viewing was done by 138 of the respondents (31.22%) and low viewing was found among 166 (37.56%) respondents.

Table 5.4: Distribution of Respondents by their Level of viewing and Gender

(N = 442)

Gender	*Heavy*		*Moderate*		*Low*		*Total*	
	No.	*%*	*No.*	*%*	*No.*	*%*	*No.*	*%*
Male	74	32.17	70	30.43	86	37.40	230	100.00
Female	64	30.19	68	32.08	80	37.73	212	100.00

Table 5.4 shows the distribution of respondents according to their level of viewing and gender. Among the male viewers, 74 (32.17%) were found to be heavy viewers, moderate viewers were 70 (30.43%) and low viewers, 86 (37.40%). In the female category, heavy viewers were 64 (30.19%), moderates were 68 (32.08%) and low viewers, 80 (37.73%). In the sample, low viewers are slightly more in number than heavy and moderate viewers.

Table 5.5: Distribution of Respondents by their Medium of Instruction at School

Medium of Instruction	*Total*	
	No.	*%*
English	317	71.88
Non-English	124	28.12
Total	441	100.00

Table 5.5 shows the distribution of respondents by their medium of instruction at school level. The English medium students were found to be 317 (71.88%), whereas non-English medium students numbered 124 (28.12%). In other words English medium students outnumbered the non-English medium students by 193 (44%).

Table 5.6: Distribution of Respondents by their Medium of Instruction at School and Gender

(N = 441)

Gender	*English*		*Non-English*		*Total*	
	No.	*%*	*No.*	*%*	*No.*	*%*
Male	145	63.32	84	36.68	229	100.00
Female	172	81.13	40	18.87	212	100.00

Note: It will be noticed that under some of the attributes the total number of respondents varies. This is because those respondents who did not respond to certain questions were automatically omitted from the total number of respondents in the analysis of those particular questions.

Table 5.6 gives the distribution of English and Non-English medium students according to the gender. Among the English medium students, the male students numbered 145 (63.32%) and female students, 172 (81.13%). That is to say that the female students with English medium outnumbered the English medium male students.

Table 5.7: Distribution of Respondents by their Medium of Instruction at College

English		*Non-English*		*Total*	
No.	*%*	*No.*	*%*	*No.*	*%*
387	90.63	40	9.37	427	100.00

It can be seen from Table 5.7 and Fig. 5.1 that, at the college level, out of 427 respondents, 387 respondents (90.63%) were studying in English medium and only 40 respondents (9.37%) were in non-English medium.

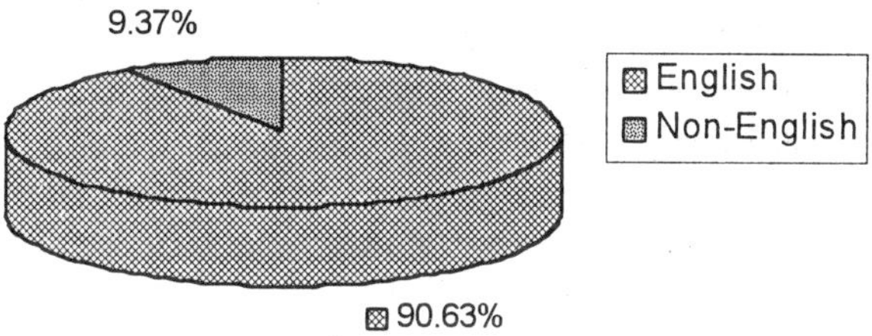

Fig. 5.1: Distribution of Respondents by their Medium of Instruction at College

Table 5.8: Distribution of Respondents by their Medium of Instruction at College and Gender

(*N* = 427)

Gender	*English*		*Non-English*		*Total*	
	No.	*%*	*No.*	*%*	*No.*	*%*
Male	190	85.97	31	14.03	221	100.00
Female	197	95.63	9	4.37	206	100.00

It can be observed from Table 5.8, that among the English medium students male respondents numbered 190 (85.97%) and female respondents 197 (95.63%). Among the 40 non-English medium students, male respondents 31 (14.03%) were in majority. Female respondents numbered only 9 (4.37%).

Table 5.9: Distribution of Respondents by their Medium of Instruction at College and Level of viewing

(*N* = *420*)

Gender	*Heavy*		*Moderate*		*Low*		*Total*	
	No.	*%*	*No.*	*%*	*No.*	*%*	*No.*	*%*
English	123	32.28	119	31.24	139	36.48	381	100.00
Non-English	9	23.08	17	33.33	17	43.59	39	100.00

Table 5.9 shows the distribution of respondents in the three categories based upon the level of viewing and their medium of instruction at college. Among the total number of 381 English medium students, the number of heavy viewers was 123 (32.28%) whereas among the total number of 39 non-English medium students, heavy viewers were found to be 9 (23.08%). It will be seen that in the matter of heavy viewing, English medium students outnumbered the non-English medium students by about 9 per cent. This may be because the FTP are in English and so English medium students are likely to comprehend these programmes better than non-English medium students.

Table 5.10: Distribution of Respondents according to Duration of having Cable Connection

(*N* = *437*)

Duration	*Total*	
	No.	*%*
Less than 1 year	79	18.04
1 year	81	18.49
2 years	64	14.62
3 years	48	10.96
4 years	74	16.89
More than 4 years	91	20.78
Total	437	100.00

The longer the duration of viewing of any Television programme, the greater may be the impact. The researcher is interested to know the spread of cable TV in general and also the association between the duration of having cable connection with viewing levels. It can be seen from the above Table 5.10, that every year on an average there is an increase by 14 per cent in cable connections.

Table 5.11: Distribution of Respondents according to Duration of having Cable connection and Level of viewing

(*N* = *433*)

Duration	*Heavy*		*Moderate*		*Low*		*Total*	
	No.	*%*	*No.*	*%*	*No.*	*%*	*No.*	*%*
Less than 1 year	17	21.50	26	32.91	36	45.56	79	100.00
1 year	23	29.48	22	28.21	33	42.31	78	100.00
2 years	31	48.44	14	21.88	19	29.68	64	100.00
3 years	16	33.33	20	41.67	12	25.00	48	100.00
4 years	16	21.92	29	39.73	28	38.35	73	100.00
More than 4 years	33	36.26	26	28.57	32	35.17	91	100.00

Table 5.11 shows no association between level of viewing and duration of having cable connection.

Is the amount of viewing related to family background such as parental education, occupation and income levels? The study looks into these issues and related data is presented below:

Table 5.12: Distribution of Respondents by their Fathers' Education

(*N* = *431*)

Education	*Total*	
	No.	*%*
Illiterate	14	03.25
High School	108	25.06
Graduate	227	52.67
Post-graduate	48	11.13
Professional	34	07.89

Table 5.12 shows the level of respondents' fathers' education. Out of 431 respondents who reported their fathers' education, a majority of 227 (52.67%) were graduates and 108 (25.06%) had high school education. Among the remaining sample, the respondents whose fathers were postgraduates numbered 48 (11.13%) and the fathers who happened to be professionals were 34 (7.89%). Only 14 (3.25%) respondents' fathers were illiterate.

Table 5.13: Distribution of Respondents by their Fathers' Education and Level of viewing

(*N* = 424)

Fathers' Education	*Heavy*		*Moderate*		*Low*		*Total*	
	No.	*%*	*No.*	*%*	*No.*	*%*	*No.*	*%*
Illiterate	5	38.46	4	30.76	4	30.76	13	100
High School	31	29.24	35	33.02	40	37.74	106	100
Graduate	76	34.08	67	30.05	80	35.87	223	100
Post-graduate	13	27.08	17	35.42	18	37.50	48	100
Professional	12	35.29	10	29.41	12	35.30	34	100

Table 5.13 reveals that there is no association between fathers' education and the level of viewing.

Table 5.14: Distribution of Respondents by their Mothers' Education

(*N* = 427)

Education	*Total*	
	No.	*%*
Illiterate	68	15.67
High School	237	54.61
Graduate	102	23.50
Post-graduate	23	5.30
Professional	4	0.92

Table 5.14 reveals that 237 respondents' (54.61%) mothers had high school education and 102 respondents' (23.50%) mothers were graduates. A very small number of respondents' mothers had either post-graduation (23) (5.30%) or a professional degree (4) (0.92%)

Table 5.15: Distribution of Respondents by their Mothers' Education and Level of viewing

(*N* = 427)

Mothers' Education	*Heavy*		*Moderate*		*Low*		*Total*	
	No.	*%*	*No.*	*%*	*No.*	*%*	*No.*	*%*
Illiterate	23	34.85	23	34.85	20	30.30	66	100
High School	71	30.60	67	28.88	94	40.52	232	100
Graduate	38	37.25	35	34.31	29	28.43	102	100
Post-graduate	4	17.39	9	39.13	10	43.48	23	100
Professional	0	0	2	50.00	2	50.00	4	100

Table 5.15 shows that there is no association between the level of viewing of respondents and respondents' mothers' education.

Table 5.16: Distribution of Respondents by their Fathers' Occupation

(*N* = *433*)

Occupation	*Total*	
	No.	*%*
Not-Working	2	0.46
Working	278	64.20
Business	115	26.56
Agriculture	38	8.78

Table 5.16 shows that a majority of 278 respondents' (64.20%) fathers are working and 115 of respondents' (26.56%) fathers are engaged in business. The remaining students' fathers numbering 38 (8.78%) are in the agricultural sector and the fathers of 2 respondents do not work anywhere.

Table 5.17: Distribution of Respondent by their Fathers' Occupation and Level of viewing

(*N* = *426*)

Occupation	*Heavy*		*Moderate*		*Low*		*Total*	
	No.	*%*	*No.*	*%*	*No.*	*%*	*No.*	*%*
Not-Working	1	50.00	0	0	1	50.00	2	100
Working	89	32.60	84	30.77	100	36.63	273	100
Business	37	32.17	34	29.56	44	38.26	115	100
Agriculture	9	25.00	15	41.67	12	33.33	36	100

Table 5.17shows that there is no association between the level of veiwing of the respondents and their fathers'occupation.

Table 5.18: Distribution of Respondents by their Mothers' Occupation

(*N* = *433*)

Occupation	*Total*	
	No.	*%*
Not-Working	377	87.07
Working	47	10.85
Business	2	0.40
Agriculture	7	1.62

Table 5.18 on mothers' occupation reveals that a majority of 377 (87.07%) respondents' mothers happened to be housewives.

Table 5.19: Distribution of Respondents by their Mothers' Occupation and Level of Viewing

(*N* = *426*)

Occupation	*Heavy*		*Moderate*		*Low*		*Total*	
	No.	*%*	*No.*	*%*	*No.*	*%*	*No.*	*%*
Not-Working	121	32.62	113	30.45	137	36.93	371	100.00
Working	14	30.435	18	39.13	14	30.435	46	100.00
Business	0	0	0	0.00	2	100.00	2	100.00
Agriculture	1	14.298	4	57.14	2	28.57	7	100.00

Table 5.19 shows that there is no association between the level of viewing of respondents and their mothers' occupation.

Table 5.20: Distribution of Respondents by their Fathers' Income

(*N* = *437*)

Income per month (Rs.)	*Total*	
	No.	*%*
Less than 3000-5000	194	44.39
5001-11,000	164	37.53
More than 11,000	79	18.08

It follows from Table 5.20 that 194 respondents (44.39%) belong to the income category of less than Rs. 5000 per month. The respondents numbering 164 (37.53%) fall in the income category of 5001-11,000 and the remaining 79 respondents (18.08%) belong to the income category of more than Rs. 11,000 per month.

Table 5.21: Distribution of Respondents by their Fathers' Income and Level of Viewing

(*N* = *430*)

Income per month (Rs.)	*Heavy*		*Moderate*		*Low*		*Total*	
	No.	*%*	*No.*	*%*	*No.*	*%*	*No.*	*%*
Less than 3000-5000	56	29.17	61	31.77	75	39.06	192	100
5001-11,000	57	37.63	47	29.37	56	35.00	160	100
More than 11,000	25	32.05	26	33.33	27	34.62	78	100

Table 5.21 shows no association between the level of viewing and the income group to which the respondents belong.

The study does not provide any evidence to support the argument that socio-economic status of the parents has an obvious influence on the amount of viewing of the student respondents. It may be because the foreign TV is a novelty to the Indian audience. Earlier the Indian viewers have very limited choice on DD which is under strict government control for a longer period. The foreign TV with its variety in programming such as sports, music, films, soap operas etc. quickly attracted both the young viewers and parents. More over a majority of students under study have come from English Medium schools. FTP are telecast in English and the language must be a strong factor in attracting the young. Hence the young people have become vivid viewers cutting the barriers of education and income status of the parents.

6

Preferences and Reactions to Foreign Television Programmes

The cable TV channels which expanded exponentially provided a strict competition to government owned TV Channel, Doordarshan. To protect itself from the onslaught of foreign TV channels, DD responded and restructured its programming policy. The competition among the various TV channels resulted in commercialisation of electronic media in the country. The maturity of commercial broadcasting substitute the entertainment for the public. Besides, the United States experiences suggest that maturation brings with it a decline in variety of viewpoints and increased protection of establishment interests. The Doordarshan which was started with intention of combined interests of development and entertainment was facing a new challenge from the commercial Television channels. The spread and popularity of foreign channels has created some confusion to the government as well as to the general public. The foreign channels had grabbed both the viewers of Doordarshan and its revenue. There is also anxiety among the public that these channels affect the young minds and their activities adversely. At this stage where the Indian viewers were exposed to different kinds of programmes, it is very essential to study the mindset of the young viewers and their reactions to FTP. Hence the main issues dealt in this study are:

1. What channels the young prefer?
2. Reasons for watching the Foreign Television channels.
3. What kind of programmes the young viewer prefer on Foreign TV?

4. Who makes the programme decisions?
5. Whether young viewers discuss with the family members what they watch on Television channels?
6. Whether viewing of Foreign TV influence the viewing of Indian channels?
7. Whether viewing of foreign channels influence the activities of young viewers?

All these issues were discussed among the moderate, heavy and low viewers and also tried to took into how male and female reacted to it.

Channel Preferences

Responses on preferences for Foreign channels *vs.* Indian channels are presented below:

Table 6.1 : Channel Preferences

Type of Channel	*Total*	
	No.	*%*
Indian	140	36.27
Foreign	246	63.73
Total	386	100.00

It is evident from Table 6.1 and Fig. 6.1 that a majority of 63.73 per cent of respondents (246 out of 386) marked foreign channels as the most preferred ones whereas 36.27 per cent of respondents (140) preferred Indian channels. It may be, therefore, concluded that the young English medium students preferred foreign channels to Indian channels.

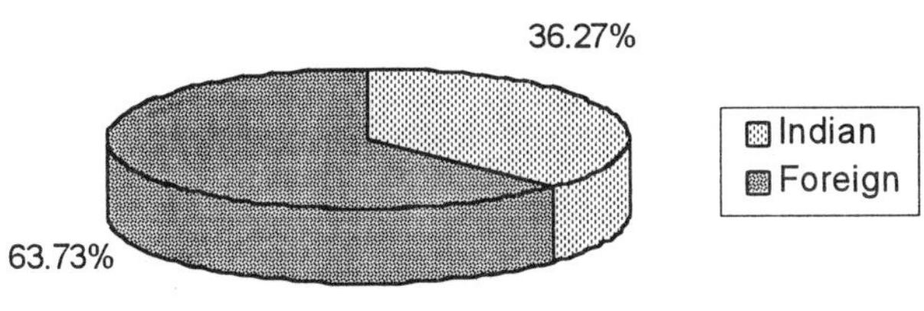

Fig. 6.1: Channel Preferences

Table 6.2: Channel Preferences and Gender

(N = 386)

Type of Channel	Indian		Foreign		Total	
	No.	%	No.	%	No.	%
Male	62	31.16	137	68.84	199	100
Female	78	41.71	109	58.29	187	100

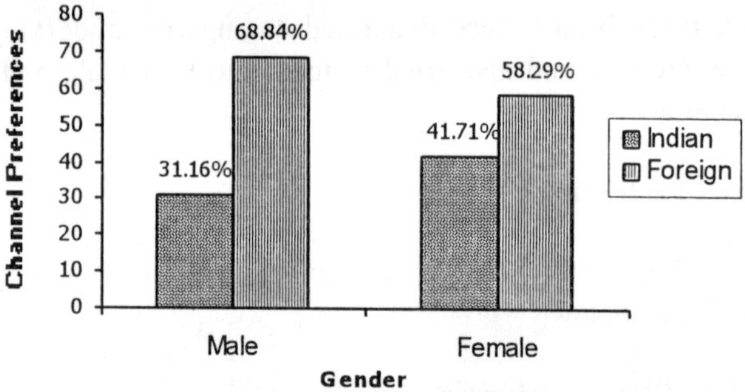

Fig. 6.2: Channel Preferences according to Gender

Table 6.2 and Fig. 6.2 show the distribution of respondents according to gender and their preference for channels. A large majority among the male respondents, *i.e.* 68.84 per cent (137 out of 199) preferred foreign channels to Indian channels. Among the female respondents, the difference between preference for foreign channels (58.2%) and that for Indian channels (41.7%) was not so wide as in the case of male respondents. Moreover, preference for foreign channels was higher (68.8%) among male respondents than among the female respondents (58.2%).

Table 6.3: Channel Preferences and Level of Viewing

(N = 382)

Level of Viewing	Indian Channels		Foreign Channels		Total	
	No.	%	No.	%	No.	%
Heavy	29	23.39	95	76.61	124	100.00
Moderate	41	35.04	76	64.95	117	100.00
Low	68	48.23	73	51.77	141	100.00

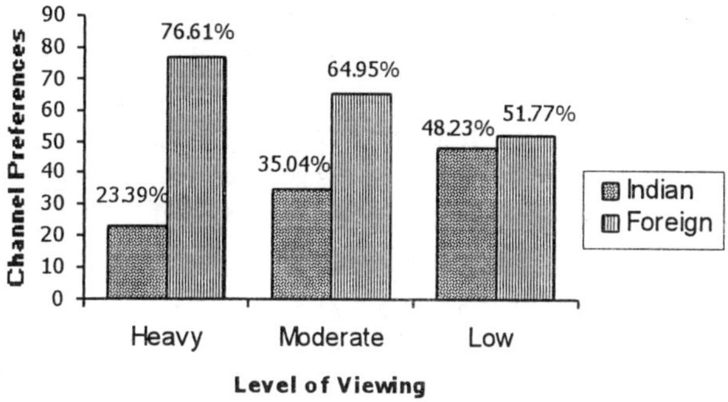

Fig. 6.3: Channel Preferences and Level of viewing

Table 6.3 and Fig. 6.3 show the association between the level of viewing and preference for channels. In the sample under study, 76.61 per cent of heavy viewers preferred foreign channels, which is higher than the moderate viewers and low viewers whose percentages are 64.95 and 51.77 respectively. Although the moderate and low viewers prefer foreign channels more than the Indian channels on the whole, their preference for Indian channels (35.0 and 48.2 per cent respectively) is found to be higher in comparison to the heavy viewers (23.4%). It can be concluded that heavy viewing of foreign television programmes may lead to a higher preference for the FTP or *vice versa*. The data clearly implies that there is a shift in preferences for channels after the FTP were introduced.

The researcher tried to analyse what makes young male and female students watch FTP. What are they looking for? Tables 6.4 and 6.5 show the reasons for watching FTP according to gender. The data indicates why they watch FTP 'always', 'sometimes' and 'rarely'. The researcher analysed the reasons for which male and female respondents watch FTP 'always' only. Among the male respondents 45.8 per cent (104) watch FTP to learn more about India and foreign countries which is greater than the female respondents whose percentage is 38.2. A second large group of 30.8 per cent of male viewers mentioned that they watch FTP to learn about others. The third largest group of male respondents mentioned that they watch FTP to forget the boredom (22.2%).

Table 6.4 : Reasons for Watching FTP—Males

Reasons	*Always*		*Sometimes*		*Rarely*		*Never*		*Total*
	No.	*%*	*No.*	*%*	*No.*	*%*	*No.*	*%*	
In relax	49	21.9	116	51.8	36	15.6	24	10.7	225
To learn about others	69	30.8	98	43.8	44	19.6	13	5.8	224
To forget the boredom of daily routine	50	22.2	92	40.9	48	21.3	35	15.6	225
To kill time/pastime	28	12.7	91	41.2	47	21.3	55	24.9	221
To discuss with others about what is viewed	31	13.8	91	40.6	54	24.1	48	21.4	224
To learn to do things not done before	37	16.5	101	45.1	55	24.6	31	13.8	224
To sit and watch with friends	41	18.2	108	48.0	51	22.7	25	11.1	225
To have variety in programmes	47	21.1	93	41.7	68	30.5	15	6.7	223
To learn more about India and foreign countries	104	45.8	72	31.7	32	14.1	19	8.4	227
To be familiar with other cultures	65	29.0	83	37.1	38	17.0	38	17.0	224

Table 6.5 : Reasons for Watching FTP—Females

Reasons	*Always*		*Sometimes*		*Rarely*		*Never*		*Total*
	No.	*%*	*No.*	*%*	*No.*	*%*	*No.*	*%*	
To relax	41	21.0	95	48.7	38	19.5	21	10.8	195
To learn about others	46	23.7	82	42.3	47	24.2	19	9.8	194
To forget the boredom of daily routine	38	20.0	78	41.1	43	22.6	31	16.3	190
To kill time/pastime	31	16.6	56	29.9	51	27.3	49	26.2	187
To discuss with others about what is viewed	25	13.7	65	35.7	39	21.4	53	29.1	182
To learn to do things not done before	33	18.9	64	36.6	34	19.4	44	25.1	175
To sit and watch with friends	23	12.8	70	39.1	55	30.7	31	17.3	179
To have variety in programmes	51	28.2	69	38.1	44	24.3	17	9.4	181
To learn more about India and Foreign countries	73	38.2	71	37.2	30	15.7	17	8.9	191
To be familiar with other cultures	52	27.1	81	42.2	37	19.3	22	11.5	192

Among the female respondents 38.2 per cent mentioned that they watch FTP to learn more about India and Foreign countries. The other two reasons, namely 'to be familiar with other cultures', 'to have variety in programmes' for which female respondents watch FTP have almost an equal percentage of viewers (27%) to their credit. The next couple of reasons, 'relaxing' and 'forgetting the boredom of daily routine' for which female respondents watch FTP also has been cited by almost an equal percentage of viewers (20%).

Tables 6.6, 6.7 and 6.8 show the association between level of viewing and reasons for watching FTP. It is interesting to note that 44.4 per cent of heavy viewers watch FTP 'to learn about others'.

The percentage of moderate and low viewers watching FTP for this reason is comparatively much less, *i.e.* 21.3 per cent and 19.1 per cent respectively. The second large group of 28.6 per cent of heavy viewers mentioned that they watch FTP to 'relax'. The number of moderate (17.3%) and low viewers (18.3%) which is again less when compared with heavy viewers. For the other reasons, there was no significant difference among the three categories of viewers.

Table 6.6 : Reasons for Watching FTP—Heavy Viewers

Reasons	*Always*		*Sometimes*		*Rarely*		*Never*		*Total*
	No.	*%*	*No.*	*%*	*No.*	*%*	*No.*	*%*	
To relax	38	28.6	60	45.1	24	18.0	11	8.3	133
To learn about others	59	44.4	49	36.8	20	15.0	5	3.8	133
To forget the boredom of daily routine	28	21.2	51	38.6	34	25.8	19	14.4	132
To kill time/pastime	15	11.6	50	38.8	28	21.7	36	27.9	129
To discuss with others about what is viewed	13	10.0	55	42.3	34	26.2	28	21.5	130
To learn to do things not done before	23	18.1	46	36.2	33	26.0	25	19.7	127
To sit and watch with friends	22	17.1	62	48.1	32	24.8	13	10.1	129
To have variety in programmes	31	24.0	52	40.3	40	31.0	6	4.7	129
To learn more about India and Foreign countries	65	50.4	41	31.8	14	10.9	9	7.0	129
To be familiar with other cultures	39	29.8	55	42.0	18	13.7	19	14.5	131

Table 6.7 : Reasons for Watching FTP—Moderate Viewers

Reasons	*Always*		*Sometimes*		*Rarely*		*Never*		*Total*
	No.	*%*	*No.*	*%*	*No.*	*%*	*No.*	*%*	
To relax	22	17.3	73	57.5	22	17.3	10	7.9	127
To learn about others	27	21.3	55	43.3	34	26.8	11	8.7	127
To forget the boredom of daily routine	29	22.5	57	44.2	23	17.8	20	15.5	129
To kill time/pastime	18	14.4	47	37.6	29	23.2	31	24.8	125
To discuss with others about what is viewed	22	18.2	45	37.2	30	24.8	24	19.8	121
To learn to do things not done before	24	20.3	55	46.6	16	13.6	23	19.5	118
To sit and watch with friends	14	11.7	59	49.2	29	24.2	18	15.0	120
To have variety in programmes	27	22.1	54	44.3	34	27.9	7	5.7	122
To learn more about India and Foreign countries	48	37.5	47	36.7	23	18.0	10	7.8	128
To be familiar with other cultures	38	30.2	47	37.3	28	22.2	13	10.3	126

Table 6.8 : Reasons for Watching FTP—Low Viewers

Reasons	*Always*		*Sometimes*		*Rarely*		*Never*		*Total*
	No.	*%*	*No.*	*%*	*No.*	*%*	*No.*	*%*	
To relax	28	18.3	76	49.7	26	17.0	23	15.0	153
To learn about others	29	19.1	72	47.4	37	24.3	14	9.2	152
To forget the boredom of daily routine	29	19.7	60	40.8	32	21.8	26	17.7	147
To kill time/pastime	25	16.9	45	30.4	41	27.7	37	25.0	148
To discuss with others about what is viewed	21	14.1	52	34.9	28	18.8	48	32.2	149
To learn to do things not done before	22	14.9	61	41.2	39	26.4	26	17.6	148
To sit and watch with friends	25	16.8	56	37.6	43	28.9	25	16.8	155
To have variety in programmes	38	25.9	55	37.4	36	24.5	18	12.2	147
To learn more about India and Foreign countries	64	41.3	52	33.5	23	14.8	16	10.3	155
To be familiar with other cultures	39	25.5	59	38.6	29	19.0	26	17.0	153

The respondents' most preferred programme on foreign channels is presented in the following tables.

Table 6.9 : Programme Preferences

Type of Programme	*Total*	
	No.	*%*
News	124	29.89
Serials	28	6.75
Feature Films	52	12.53
Interviews	4	0.96
Talk Shows	10	2.41
Documentary	1	0.24
Educational	36	8.67
Quiz	19	4.58
Sports	54	13.01
Music	82	19.76
Human Interest Stories	5	1.20
Total	415	100.00

One of the reasons for the popularity of foreign channels is the availability of a wide choice in their programming. We looked at which programmes on foreign channels appeal to the respondents. The findings are presented in Table 6.9. Respondents were asked to mark three programmes in the order of their preference. While analysing the responses, only the first choice is taken into consideration as their most preferred choice. A wide variety of programmes were indicated by the respondents as their second and third choices. So, the researcher decided to focus on the respondents' programme of first choice and ignore the second and third choices to avoid the ambiguity and confusion which might result by ascribing differential values to their choices and making calculations on the basis of it. It is noticed that 29.89 per cent respondents preferred news, followed by music (19.76%), sports (13.01%) and feature films (12.53%). It may be concluded that the respondents in general are looking for news and entertainment, which include music, sports and feature films.

Table 6.10 : Programme Preferences and Gender

(N = 415)

Type of Programme	Male		Female	
	No.	%	No.	%
News	71	32.27	53	27.18
Serials	10	4.55	18	9.23
Feature Films	34	15.45	18	9.23
Interviews	1	0.45	3	1.54
Talk Shows	2	0.91	8	4.10
Documentary	0	0.00	1	0.51
Educational	23	10.46	13	6.67
Quiz	8	3.64	11	5.64
Sports	39	17.73	15	7.69
Music	29	13.18	53	27.18
Human Interest Stories	3	1.36	2	1.03
Total	220	100.00	195	100.00

Table 6.10 shows an association between the gender and the preference for a specific programme on FTP. Among the males 32.27 per cent of respondents preferred news, which is followed by sports (17.73%) and feature films (15.45%). In the case of the female respondents 27.18 per cent preferred news and music programmes equally, followed by serials and feature films (9.23%) equally.

Table 6.11 : Programme Preferences and Level of Viewing

(N = 412)

Programme Type	Heavy		Moderate		Low	
	No.	%	No.	%	No.	%
News	32	24.06	47	35.88	44	29.73
Serials	8	6.02	9	6.87	11	7.43
Feature Films	22	16.54	13	9.92	17	11.48
Interviews	0	0.00	1	0.76	3	2.03
Talk Shows	5	3.76	2	1.53	3	2.03
Documentary	0	0.00	0	0.00	1	0.68
Educational	12	9.02	10	7.63	13	8.78
Quiz	5	3.76	10	7.63	4	2.70
Sports	18	13.53	14	10.69	21	14.19
Music	31	23.31	23	17.56	28	18.92
Human Interest Stories	0	0.00	2	1.53	3	2.03
Total	133	100.00	131	100.00	148	100.00

Table 6.11 shows an association between the level of viewing and preference for specific programmes. Proportionately a large number of

moderate (35.88%) and low viewers (29.73%) gave their first preference for news programmes than the heavy viewers (24.06%). Heavy viewers were found to be watching more entertainment oriented programmes like music (23.31%), feature films (16.54%) more than moderate and low viewers. Sports programmes were found to be the first choice by the fourth largest group of respondents across the level of viewing.

Respondents mentioned varied programmes as their first choice. The researcher was interested in finding out the kind of programmes which young viewers were comparatively more interested in. The researcher decided to classify the programmes included in the schedule into two categories; information oriented and entertainment oriented. The programmes like news, interviews, talk shows, documentary, educational, quiz, human interest stories were clubbed together as information oriented and the remaining programmes, namely serials, feature films, sports and music were combined as entertainment oriented programmes. The preferences indicated by th respondents were calculated according to the classification. The results according to gender distribution are presented in Table 6.12 and Figure 6.4.

Table 6.12 : Preferences for either Information or Entertainment and Gender

(*N* = *415*)

Gender	*Information*		*Entertainment*		*Total*	
	No.	*%*	*No.*	*%*	*No.*	*%*
Male	108	49.09	112	50.91	220	100.00
Female	91	46.67	104	53.33	195	100.00

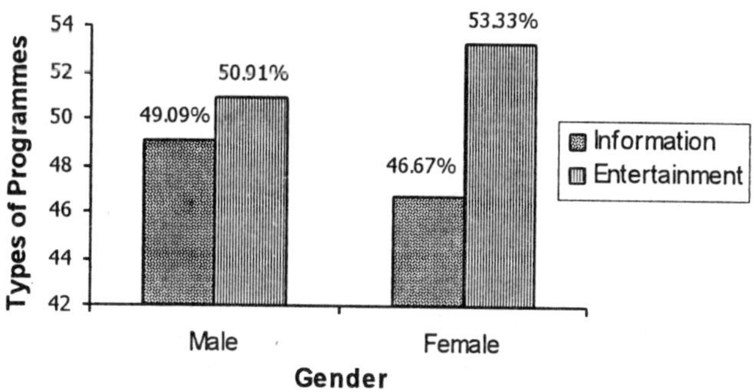

Fig. 6.4: Preferences for either Information or Entertainment and Gender

From Table 6.12 and Fig. 6.4, it was found that male respondents gave almost equal preference to information and entertainment whereas female respondents gave more preference to entertainment than information. In the case of male respondents, the figures were 49 per cent and 51 per cent respectively whereas in the case of female viewers, the percentages were 47 and 53 respectively.

Table 6.13: Preference for either Information or Entertainment and Level of Viewing

(*N* = *412*)

Level of Viewing	*Information*		*Entertainment*		*Total*	
	No.	*%*	*No.*	*%*	*No.*	*%*
Heavy	54	40.60	79	59.40	133	100.00
Moderate	72	54.96	59	45.04	131	100.00
Low	71	47.97	77	52.03	148	100.00

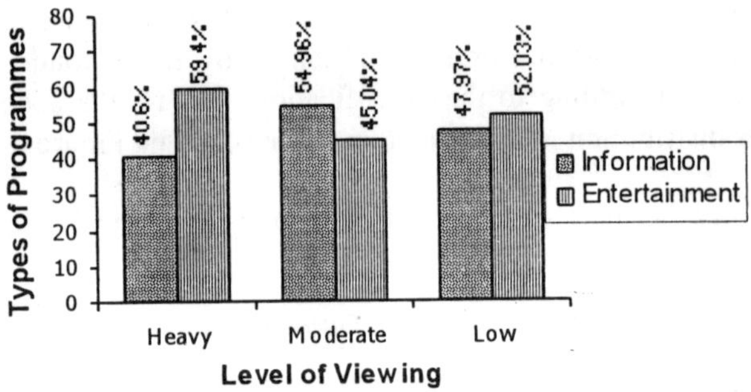

Fig. 6.5: Preference for either Information or Entertainment and Level of Viewing

Table 6.13 and Fig. 6.5 show a strong association between level of viewing and preference for entertainment programmes. Among the 133 heavy viewers, 59.40 per cent of respondents preferred entertainment whereas 40.60 per cent of respondents preferred information oriented programmes. In the case of moderate viewers, the preferential order was found to be reversed. They preferred information-oriented programmes to the entertainment programmes. Among the 131 moderate viewers, 54.96 per cent of respondents preferred information and 45.04 per cent of respondents preferred entertainment oriented programmes. Further, in the case of low viewers it was found that the difference between preference for information and entertainment programmes was marginal. Out of 148 low viewers, 47.97 per cent of respondents preferred information oriented programmes where as 52.03 per cent of respondents preferred entertainment programmes.

Table 6.14: Persons who make Programme Decisions

Deciding Person	*Total*	
	No.	*%*
Father	37	8.58
Mother	14	3.25
Respondent	96	22.28
Sister	13	3.02
Brother	22	5.10
Anybody	249	57.77
Total	431	100.00

Although the programme decisions are related to a number of factors like nature of programmes, telecast timings, and interests of family members, it is mainly indicative of power relations within the family. The most powerful member among those who are present at the time of viewing is found usually to decide which programme is to be watched. The researcher wanted to see the extent to which this assumption is found to be valid. The results are shown in Table 6.14. In the sample, in general, a majority of 57.77 per cent of respondents (249) said there is no control on who decides which programme is to be watched in the family and anyone of the family members can decide. However, 22.88 per cent of respondents (96) mentioned that they were the decision-makers of the programme to be watched on foreign channels. And among the remaining, 8.58 per cent of respondents (37) mentioned that the fathers decide and they were followed by brothers, *i.e.* 5.10 per cent (22) mothers, 3.25 per cent (14) and sisters 3.02 per cent (13). It can be concluded therefore, that the male members are playing a dominating role than the female members. The fathers and the brothers put together (37+22 = 59) outnumbered the mothers and sisters put together (14+13 = 27). The data presented in Table 6.15 further proves this.

Table 6.15 : Persons who make Programme Decisions and Gender

(N = 431)

Deciding Person	*Male*		*Female*	
	No.	*%*	*No.*	*%*
Father	15	6.67	22	10.68
Mother	12	5.33	2	0.97
Respondent	61	27.11	35	16.99
Sister	5	2.22	8	3.88
Brother	8	3.56	14	6.80
Anybody	124	55.11	125	60.68
Total	225	100.00	206	100.00

Table 6.15 indicates that a majority of 55.11 per cent of male respondents (124) and 60.68 per cent of female respondents (125) claimed that there was no strict control on who should make decisions in the family with regard to FTP viewing. If we keep them aside and look at the remaining male and female respondents, an interesting indicator of power relations in the family emerges.

It is seen that 27.11 per cent of male respondents (61) as against 16.99 per cent of female respondents (35) said that they themselves made decisions about the programme to be watched. Similarly fathers and brothers together (15+8 = 23) as against mothers and sisters put together (12+5 = 17) decided which programmes were to be watched in the case of male respondents. It is interesting to note that in the case of female respondents, fathers and brothers put together (22+14 = 36) against the mothers and sisters (2+8 = 10) decided the programme on FTP. These figures clearly indicate that there is a pronounced association between gender and decision-making in the family. It can be said that it is mostly the male member in the family who takes the decisions with regard to TV viewing.

Table 6.16 : Persons who make Programme Decisions and Level of Viewing

(*N* = *428*)

Deciding Person	*Heavy*		*Moderate*		*Low*	
	No.	*%*	*No.*	*%*	*No.*	*%*
Father	11	8.21	9	6.77	17	10.75
Mother	4	2.99	5	3.76	5	3.16
Respondent	39	29.10	22	16.54	33	20.89
Sister	2	1.49	2	1.50	9	5.70
Brother	9	6.72	4	3.01	9	5.70
Anybody	69	51.49	91	68.42	85	53.80
Total	137	100.00	133	100.00	158	100.00

Table 6.16 shows the association between level of viewing and decision-making person about FTP viewing. The table under discussion provides an additional interesting factor. It is noticed that heavy viewers (29.10%) more than moderate (16.54%) and low viewers (20.89%) are decision-makers with regard to FTP. This may probably be because heavy viewing involves personal decisions rather than decisions taken by others.

Table 6.17: The Basis of Programme Related Discussions

Discussion	*Total*	
	No.	*%*
Always	198	46.70
Sometimes	36	8.49
Rarely	52	12.26
Never	103	24.29
Depends on Programme	35	8.25
Total	425	100.00

Table 6.17 shows the programme related discussion with family members on FTP.

Apprehension has been expressed that TV viewing weakens the relations among the members of a family because it tends to replace interactions among them. Moreover men and women are claimed to react differently to TV messages. Men are said to watch TV more attentively whereas women were reported to combine TV viewing with other activities such as household chores and conversation (Morley, 1988). Most importantly, discussion of TV programmes with members of the family and peers is reported to play a significant role in the impact of TV programmes on individual viewers. It gives an understanding about what meanings the individual members give to these TV messages, what pleasures they derive and how they use them in real life. Therefore an attempt was made to find out whether young viewers included in the sample discuss the programmes that they watch with other members of the family. In the sample 46.70 per cent of respondents (198) mentioned that they always discuss about the programmes with the family members as against 24.29 per cent of respondents (103) who mentioned that they never discussed them with them.

Table 6.18: Programme Related Discussion and Gender

(*N = 424*)

Discussion	*Male*		*Female*	
	No.	*%*	*No.*	*%*
Always	90	39.65	108	54.82
Sometimes	26	11.45	10	5.08
Rarely	32	14.10	20	10.15
Never	65	28.63	38	19.29
Depends on Programme	14	6.17	21	10.66
Total	227	100.00	197	100.00

Table 6.18 reveals an association between gender and discussion of the programmes with other members of the family. Out of 197 female viewers, 54.82 per cent of respondents (108) reported that they always discussed the FTP programmes with the members of the family. As against this only 19.29 per cent of female members (38) never discussed the FTP programmes. On the other hand, out of 227 males, 39.65 per cent of respondents (90) said that they always discussed the FTP with the members in the family. As against this 28.63 per cent of male respondents (65) who asserted that they never discussed with members in the family. It may be concluded that women are more attached to the family than the boys and that they like to share with the family their impressions and experiences.

Table 6.19: Programmes Related Discussion and Level of Viewing

(*N* = *418*)

Discussion	*Heavy*		*Moderate*		*Low*	
	No	*%*	*No*	*%*	*No*	*%*
Always	63	47.73	70	52.63	63	41.18
Sometimes	14	10.61	12	9.02	9	5.98
Rarely	10	7.57	17	12.78	25	16.34
Never	35	26.52	27	20.30	40	26.14
Depends on Programme	10	7.57	7	5.27	16	10.40
Total	132	100.00	133	100.00	153	100.00

Table 6.19 establishes no association between viewing levels of FTP and discussion of programmes by the respondents with the family members.

Table 6.20: Impact of FTP Viewing on the Duration of Viewing of Indian Channels

Impact	*Total*	
	No.	*%*
Decreased	179	43.24
Remained same	171	41.30
Increased	64	15.46
Total	414	100.00

Table 6.20 and Fig. 6.6 present the data on the impact of viewing of FTP on the viewing of Indian channels. Among the total number of 414 respondents, 43.24 per cent of respondents (179) reported that the duration of viewing of Indian television channels decreased as a result of FTP. In the remaining sample, 41.30 per cent of respondents (171)

said their viewing of Indian channels remained unaffected and only 15.46 per cent of respondents (64) reported increased viewing of Indian channels. The results clearly indicate that the foreign television channels have cut down the viewership of Indian channels.

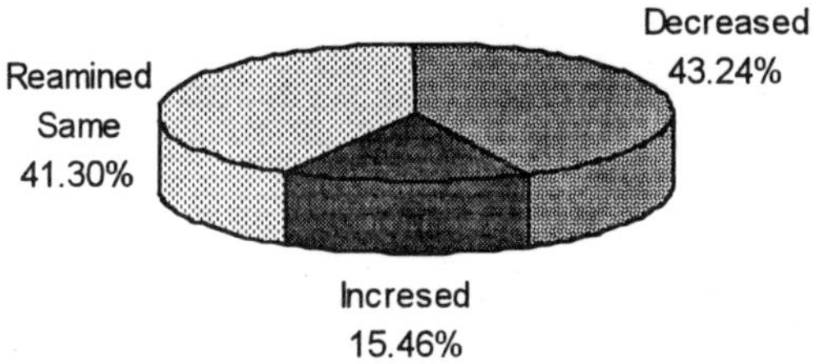

Fig. 6.6: Impact of FTP Viewing on the Duration of Viewing of Indian Channels

Table 6.21: Impact of FTP Viewing on the Duration of Viewing of Indian Channels and Gender

(*N = 414*)

Gender	*Decreased*		*Remained Same*		*Increased*		*Total*	
	No.	*%*	*No.*	*%*	*No.*	*%*	*No.*	*%*
Male	108	50.46	68	31.78	38	17.76	214	100.00
Female	71	35.50	103	51.50	26	13.00	200	100.00

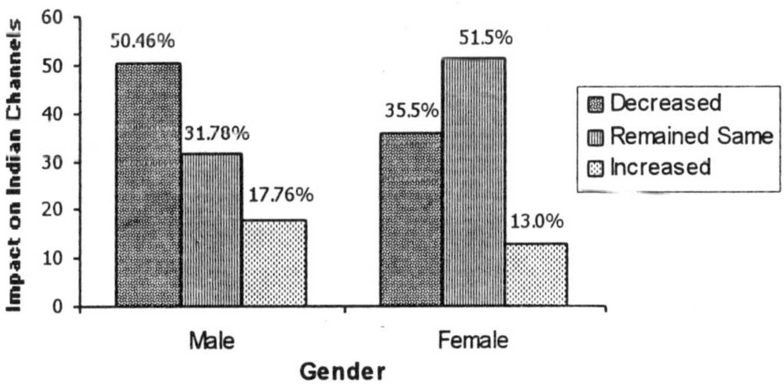

Fig. 6.7: Impact of FTP Viewing on the Duration of Viewing of Indian Channels and Gender

Table 6.21 and Fig. 6.7 discuss the impact of viewing of foreign channels on the viewing of Indian channels according to the gender. Among the 179 respondents who reported that the duration of their viewing of Indian channels decreased, 50.46 per cent of respondents (108) were males and 35.50 per cent of respondents (71) were females. Among those who mentioned that the viewing of Indian channels remained the same even after watching the foreign channels, it is again the male respondents whose percentage is less, *i.e.* 31.78 than the female respondents whose percentage is 51.50.

Table 6.22: Impact of FTP Viewing on the Duration of Viewing of Indian Channels and Level of Viewing

(*N* = *409*)

Impact	*Heavy*		*Moderate*		*Low*	
	No.	*%*	*No.*	*%*	*No.*	*%*
Decreased	73	54.89	44	35.20	62	41.06
Remained same	40	30.07	61	48.80	67	49.37
Increased	20	15.04	20	16.00	22	14.52
Total	133	100.00	125	100.00	151	100.00

It can be observed from Table 6.22 that duration of viewing of Indian channels is affected due to the FTP. The percentage of heavy viewers (54.89%) who have mentioned that viewing of Indian channels has decreased is higher than that of moderate (35.20%) and low viewers (41.06%). Nearly half of the respondents in moderate and low viewers' category mentioned that their viewing of Indian channels remained unaffected. The data in the study clearly indicates an association between viewing of FTP and its impact on the viewing of Indian channels.

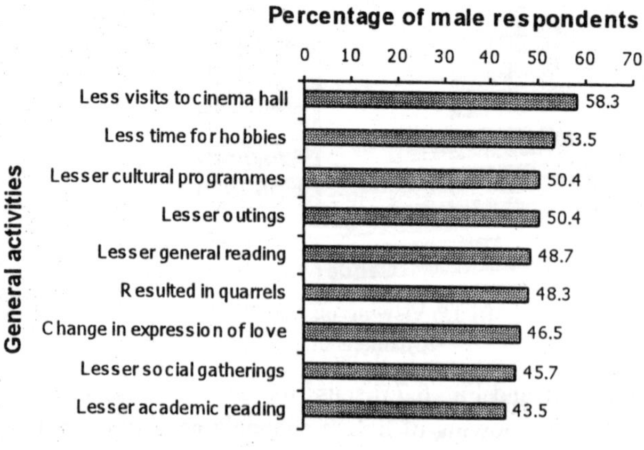

Fig. 6.8: Influence of FTP on General Activities—Males

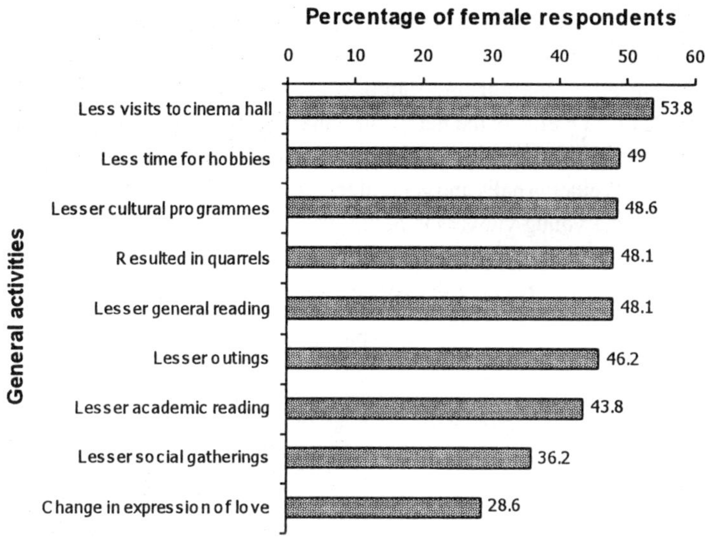

Fig. 6.9: Influence of FTP on General Activities—Females

A number of questions were posed to find out whether viewing of FTP influences the general activity of the respondents. Figures 6.8 and 6.9 show the association between the FTP and its impact on the general activities of the respondents according to gender. The data is presented using Sorted Histogram which highlights the dominating parameters that are being affected. Each figure shows the percentage of response as a horizontal bar against the general activity.

The most obvious implication was that both male (58.30%) and female respondents (53.80%) reported decreased viewing of films at the cinema halls. Another prominent difference between male and female viewers is found in the changes in the expression of love and affection like kissing and hugging. Among the male viewers 46.5 per cent have mentioned that FTP influenced the modes of expression of love and affection whereas only 28.6 per cent of female respondents said 'yes' to it. The admission made by the male viewers that the modes of expression of love and affection had changed as a result of FTP viewing is a clear indication that the behavioural patterns of the young viewers are undergoing a change and it may eventually be so in the case of females. Although at the moment it had happened in the case of only 28.6 per cent of them.

On the whole the study implies that nearly fifty per cent of both male and female respondents reported that their outings, general reading and attending other cultural programmes are affected. Thus it is clear that viewing of FTP affects the male and female viewers in a variety of ways. The reduction in time allotted for hobbies, cultural programmes, outings and visits to cinema halls and general reading etc., indicates that the cultural aspect of the young viewers is being affected. What will be the result of such an impact cannot be known now. But it can be safely summarised that the cultural aspects of the young viewers will eventually be affected.

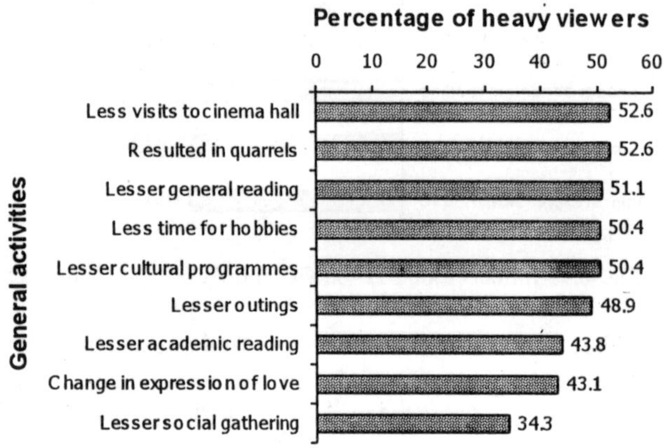

Fig. 6.10: Influence of FTP on General Activities—Heavy Viewers

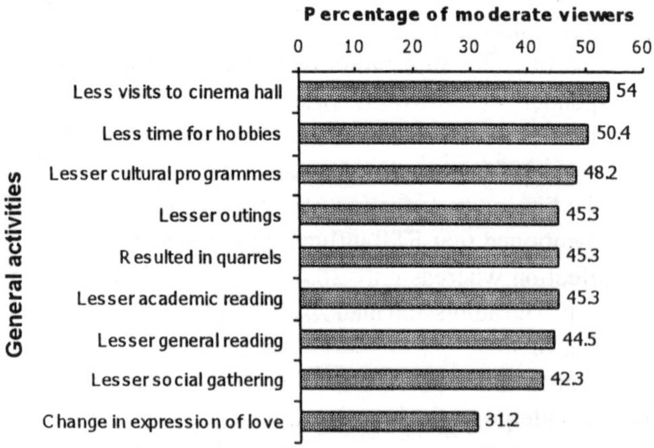

Fig. 6.11: Influence of FTP on General Activities—Moderate Viewers

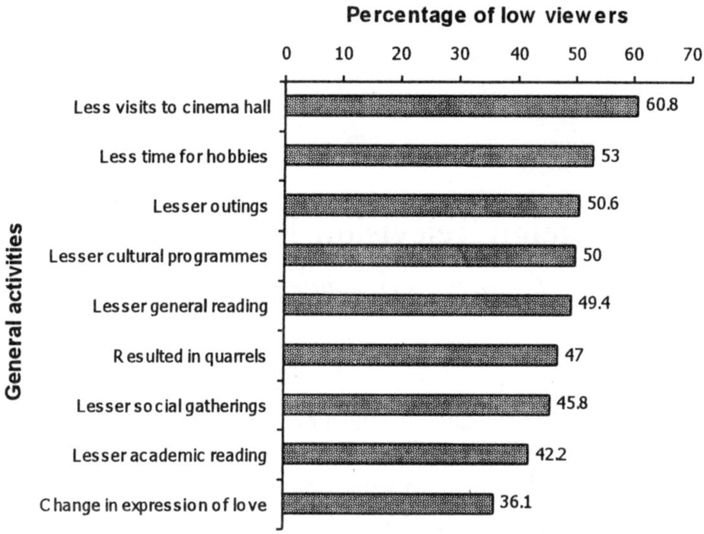

Fig. 6.12: Influence of FTP on General Activities—Low Viewers

Figures 6.10, 6.11 and 6.12 show the influence of FTP on the general activities of the respondents according to level of viewing. Foreign television programming does make much difference among the three categories of viewers, *i.e.* heavy, moderate and low, with regards to outings, social and other cultural groupings and general reading. But with regards to changes in expression of love and affection and going to pubs, heavy viewers reacted more positively than moderate and low viewers. Slightly a large percentage of heavy viewers (43.1%) than that of the moderate (31.2%) and low viewers (36.1%) mentioned that their ways of expressing love and affection had changed.

7

Foreign Television Programmes

Change in Attitudes of Youth

India experienced the sudden and unregulated growth of satellite channels since 1990. These channels faced major criticism that the programmes implant western values on young minds. Concern was expressed over the volume of sex and violence based entertainment received which was not basically intended for Indian viewers. It was considered that values and lifestyles depicted in these programmes could affect the youth socially and culturally in many ways.

The values influence the thinking and shape the lifestyle of people. Persons and Shills (1962) define value as the orientation of individuals whereby one committed to the observation of certain norms, standards and criteria of selection. The values are inseparable from attitudes and sometimes overlap each other (Johnson, 1960).

The young people in the age group of 18-22 years are vulnerable to the outside influence where TV plays a vital role in formulating the opinion on various issues. How do the young people react to the foreign programming which depicts family relations, women roles, lifestyles, sex norms etc., in a different manner from the Indian system? What are their reactions to the soap operas, chat shows, films, music programmes etc., on these foreign channels? Do the western norms in FTP set a socio-cultural agenda for the young ? Do the young viewers' attitudes change due to their constant exposure to foreign programming? Keeping these factors in mind five major issues were dealt in the present research. They are:

1. The relationship between the heavy viewing of FTP and acceptance of western family norms.

2. The relationship between the heavy viewing of FTP and change in attitudes towards social roles of Indian women.
3. The relationship between heavy viewing of FTP and change in attitudes towards sex norms.
4. The relationship between heavy viewing of FTP and change in attitudes towards lifestyles.
5. The relationship between heavy viewing of FTP and change in attitudes towards western music.

In tune with the above issues ten hypotheses have been formulated to test the relationship between exposure to Foreign Television Programmes (the independent variable) and acceptance of western norms (the dependent variable). Sample data has been analysed separately to examine each hypothesis. The major statistical tool used is MANOVA. MANOVA is a multivariate procedure that handles the comparison of means of several dependent variables at a time with respect to groups.

Evaluating Attitudes towards Western Norms

Each of the five dependent variables is operationalised into a set of parameters to each of which the answers are obtained on a Likert 5-point scale as follows:

Opinion	*Value*
Strongly Agree	5
Agree	4
Undecided	3
Somewhat disagree	2
Strongly disagree	1

For each respondent the mean response score on each question was calculated with respect to the selected group or category. If the mean score is close to 5, it indicates acceptance of western norm and if it is close to 1 it indicates rejection of western norm. In order to have a criterion for classification of respondents according to their opinions, we have used the following cut-off values:

Mean Score	*Opinion*
1.00 – 2.50	Rejection of Western Norm
2.51 – 3.50	Undecided
3.51 – 5.00	Acceptance of Western Norm

Since the response to each question is likely to differ according to the level of viewing and gender, a multivariate statistical tool known as Multivariate Analysis of Variance (MANOVA) has been used to compare the mean scores of the group of questions with respect to the above two factors.

Western Norms

Family norms (17 Items)	Social roles (13 Items)	Sexual norms (10 Items)	Lifestyles (10 Items)	Music preferences (9 Items)

For the purpose of this study, the construct "Western norms" has been conceptualised as having 5 dimensions: Family norms, Social roles of Indian women, Sexual norms, Lifestyles and Music preferences. Each dimension is operationalised into a set of dependent variables. The dimension of family norms has 17 dependent variables, the dimension of social roles of Indian women has 13 items, the dimension of sexual norms has 10 items, the dimension of lifestyles has 10 items, and the dimension of music preferences has 9 items.

The results of MANOVA for each hypothesis are summarised in the following sections in the order of the hypotheses being tested.

WESTERN FAMILY NORMS

Hypothesis-1

> "Young heavy viewers of foreign television programmes tend to show a greater degree of acceptance of Western family norms than moderate and low viewers of foreign television programmes."

The homogeneity of the co-variance matrices assumption appeared to be violated. In the present study, th outcome of the Box's M test F (303662) DF = 1.20570, p = 0.016 (approx.) test was disregarded due to three reasons: the cell sizes were roughly equal and above 30; the test is notably sensitive to violations of normality (Norusis, 1990) and, the Pillai's test statistic was chosen for the MANOVA procedure. Olson (1976) recommends the use of Pillai's test because it is the most robust of the invariant tests and is sufficiently powerful to detect population differences in any non-centrality structure.

The independent variable is the foreign television programmes viewing with three levels (heavy, moderate and low). The dimension of family norms is operationalised into a set of 17 dependent variables. MANOVA has been carried out among the three categories of viewers. The following are the results:

Table 7.1: Results of MANOVA Test of Significant Difference Between the Three Categories of Viewers of Foreign Television Programmes on Family Norms

(*N = 350*)

Test Name	*Value*	*Exact F*	*Hypoth. DF*	*Error DF*	*Sig. of F*
Pillai's	0.08627	1.00378	30.00	668.00	0.462
Hotelling's	0.09026	0.99888	30.00	664.00	0.470
Wilk's	0.91555	1.00133	30.00	666.00	0.466
Roy's	0.04978				

The hypothesis is not supported. Table 7.1 indicates no statistically significant difference among the three categories of viewers on the dimension of Family norms.

Hypothesis-2

> "Because of heavy viewing of foreign television programmes, young male viewers tend to show a greater degree of acceptance of Western family norms than young female viewers."

The homogeneity has not been violated as shown by Box's M test, F (153.34060) DF = 1.16992, p = 0.074 (approx.).

Table 7.2: Results of MANOVA Test of Significant Difference Between Young Male and Female Heavy Viewers on the Western Family Norms

(N-127)

Test Name	*Value*	*Exact F*	*Hypoth. DF*	*Error DF*	*Sig. of F*
Pillai's	0.32208	2.54313	17.00	91.00	0.002
Hotelling's	0.47509	2.54313	17.00	91.00	0.002
Wilk's	0.67792	2.54313	17.00	91.00	0.002
Roy's	0.32208				

The MANOVA test indicates a significant difference between young male and female heavy viewers on the set of 17 dependent variables of Family norms. Pillai's criterion indicated that combined dependent variables were influenced by the level of exposure of foreign television programmes (p = 0.002). Thus MANOVA test indicates a significant difference between young male and female heavy viewers.

Univariate F-tests were performed to identify the individual variables for which the mean scores differ significantly with respect to young male and female heavy viewers. Univariate F-tests were carried out on the scores and the results are presented in Table 7.3.

The perceived significant difference between young male and female heavy viewers was found on two out of the seventeen dependent variables. They are: 'mother must be consulted' and 'self-choice marriages last longer than arranged marriages'. No other dependent variable of family norms differed significantly for young male and female heavy viewers. In order to determine whether the young male heavy viewers acceptance of Western family norms is greater than that of the female heavy viewers, mean scores were examined, the results of which are presented below.

The perceived difference between the young male and female heavy viewers was found with respect to:

1. 'Mother must be consulted in decision making'
   Mean score for male heavy viewers: 4.04
   Mean score for female heavy viewers: 4.43
2. 'Self-choice marriages last longer than arranged marriages'
   Mean score for male heavy viewers: 3.60
   Mean score for female heavy viewers: 3.00

Table 7.3 : Results of Univariate F-tests of Western Family Norms

Variables	*Hypoth. SS*	*Error SS*	*Hypoth MS*	*Error MS*	*F*	*Sig. of F*
Decision by father not by mother	1.60337	229.31406	1.60337	2.14312	0.74815	0.389
Mother to be consulted	**2.33676**	**55.40636**	**2.33676**	**0.51782**	**4.51273**	**0.036**
Young people must have a say	1.29833	96.66498	1.29833	0.90341	1.43714	0.233
Father deciding the career	0.62249	189.06558	0.62249	1.76697	0.35229	0.554
Father decisions by young people	0.33776	190.26775	0.33776	1.77820	0.18994	0.664
The young depending on parents economically	0.02741	241.11021	0.02741	2.25337	0.01216	0.912
The young should be financially independent	2.22506	92.49053	2.22506	0.86440	2.57412	0.112
The young must obey elders	0.44316	126.54767	0.44316	1.18269	0.37470	0.542
The young must use polite language	1.59002	117.69439	1.59002	1.09995	1.44554	0.232
The young can argue with parents	1.37983	154.65686	1.37983	1.44539	0.95464	0.331
The young have to take care of parents	0.16407	109.52400	0.16407	1.02359	0.16029	0.690
Arranged marriages are better	2.58534	153.17613	2.58534	1.43155	1.80597	0.182
Self-choice marriages last longer	**9.39018**	**158.35294**	**9.39018**	**1.47993**	**6.34500**	**0.013**
Marriage rituals should be scrapped	0.03227	189.93103	0.03227	1.77506	0.01818	0.893
Civil marriage is better	0.82580	148.42191	0.82580	1.38712	0.59533	0.442
Living together without marriage is valid	5.37140	171.60108	5.37140	1.60375	3.34928	0.070
Nuclear family gives more happiness	1.43837	159.60751	1.43831	1.49166	0.96427	0.328

The results given above indicate that the young male heavy viewers of FTP have scored higher mean scores than the young female heavy viewers, which implies a greater acceptance of Western family norms by males than females. Hence, the hypothesis is partially supported. Male heavy viewers showed greater acceptance of self-choice marriages whereas female heavy viewers, showed greater acceptance of the opinion: 'mother to be consulted.'

From the mean scores, it can be seen that young female heavy viewers strongly agreed that mother must be consulted in decision-making and male heavy viewers tend to merely agree with the statement. Generally the Indian families are patriarchal in nature where mother's involvement in family decisions tends to be very limited. The study gives a clear impression that perceptions about women's role in the family are undergoing a change. The results in the study indicate changing perceptions of the younger generation who want the mothers also to be equally involved in decision-making.

Young male heavy viewers tend to accept the dependent variable 'self-choice marriages last longer than arranged marriages', and females are undecided about it. The analysis indicates that heavy viewing of FTP on the part of males is leading them to the acceptance of certain Western norms like self-choice marriages. On the other hand, heavy viewing of FTP on the part of females is pushing them into a dilemma on the question of self-choice marriages.

In Indian families, marriage decisions are taken by the parents and the boy/girl together. The parents extend both moral and financial support to their son/daughter if the marriage fails and results in a divorce. This is possible only if the marriages are arranged by the parents. The girls in general are afraid of consequences of a failed marriage. The girl has to lead a life as a divorcee if she doesn't get married again. Indian girls are aware that a divorcee doesn't command respect in the society and has to face a number of unsavoury situations and comments. If the marriage is arranged by parents, the girl is supported by family members reducing the possibility of tensions that a divorcee has to face. So, even if the girl would like to go in for self-choice marriages, she thinks twice and wouldn't like to give up a sense of protection offered by the arranged marriages. This is reflected in expressing their opinion on self-choice of marriages where they are undecided about it. On the other hand male members do not face any of these problems and could therefore expressed their inclination in favour of self-choice marriages.

WESTERN SOCIAL ROLES FOR INDIAN WOMEN

Hypothesis-3

> "Young heavy viewers of foreign television programmes tend to show a greater degree of acceptance of Western social roles for Indian women than moderate and low viewers of foreign television programmes."

The homogeneity of the co-variance matrices assumption appeared to be violated. In the present study, the outcome of the Box's M Test F (182,392958) DF = 1.23261, p = 0.018 (approx.) was disregarded due to three reasons: the cell sizes were roughly equal and above 30; the test is notably sensitive to violations of normality (Norusis, 1990) and, the Pillai's test statistic was chosen for the MANOVA procedure. Olson (1976) recommends the use of Pillai's test because it is the most robust of the invariant tests and is sufficiently powerful to detect population differences in any non-centrality structure.

Table 7.4: Results of MANOVA Test of Significant Difference Between the Three Categories of Viewers of Foreign Television Programmes about the Western Social Roles for Indian Women

(*N* = *391*)

Test Name	*Value*	*Exact F*	*Hypoth. DF*	*Error DF*	*Sig. of F*
Pillai's	0.08601	1.30323	26.00	754.00	0.144
Hotelling's	0.08992	1.29686	26.00	750.00	0.148
Wilk's	0.91582	1.30004	26.00	752.00	0.146
Roy's	0.04706				

No significant difference was found among the heavy, moderate and low viewers with regard to social roles of Indian women. Thus the hypothesis is not statistically supported (p = 0.144).

Hypothesis-4

> "Because of heavy viewing of foreign television programmes, young female viewers tend to show a greater degree of acceptance of Western social roles for Indian women than young male viewers."

The homogeneity of the co-variance matrices assumption appeared to be violated. In the present study, the outcome of the Box's M test

F (91,46990) DF = 1.38679, p = 0.009 (approx.) was disregarded due to three reasons: the cell sizes were roughly equal and above 30; the test is notably sensitive to violations of normality (Norusis, 1990) and, the Pillai's test statistic was chosen for the MANOVA procedure. Olson (1976) recommends the use of Pillai's test because it is the most robust of the invariant tests and is sufficiently powerful to detect population differences in any non-centrality structure.

Table 7.5: Results of MANOVA Test of Significant Difference Between Young Male and Female Heavy Viewers of Foreign Television Programmes on the Western Social Roles of Indian Women

(N-127)

Test Name	*Value*	*Exact F*	*Hypoth. DF*	*Error DF*	*Sig. of F*
Pillai's	0.26090	3.06841	13	113	0.001
Hotelling's	0.35300	3.06841	13	113	0.001
Wilk's	0.73910	3.06841	13	113	0.001
Roy's	0.026090				

The MANOVA test indicates a significant difference between young male and female heavy viewers on a set of 13 dependent variables of Western social roles of Indian women. Pillai's criterion indicated that combined dependent variables were influenced by the level of exposure of foreign television programmes (p = 0.001).

In order to determine on which aspects young female heavy viewers differ significantly from male heavy viewers. Univariate F-tests were conducted. The mean scores of young male and female heavy viewers with respect to social roles of Indian women are presented in Table 7.6.

Table 7.6 shows statistically significant difference between young male and female heavy viewers with respect to four out of thirteen dependent variables of social roles of Indian women, namely 'economic independence', 'sharing of family work by both husband and wife', 'assertion by women of their own rights' and 'the roles of man and woman as income-generator and home-maker' respectively.

The mean scores with respect to these dependent variables are presented below:

1. 'Women must be economically independent'
   Male heavy : 3.34
   Female heavy : 4.20

Table 7.6: Results of Univariate F-tests for Social roles of Indian Women

Variables	*Hypoth. SS*	*Error SS*	*Hypoth. MS*	*Error MS*	*F*	*Sig. of F*
A woman to be a good house-wife than a successful career	5.72547	233.45563	5.72547	1.86765	3.06561	0.082
Career is not important for a woman	.75930	299.96510	.75930	2.39972	.31641	0.575
Marriage bestows respectability on a woman	.89952	183.52567	.89952	1.46821	.61267	0.435
Single woman doesn't command respect	1.22797	265.08699	1.22797	2.12070	.57904	0.448
A woman has to take care of children	2.71887	217.02916	2.71887	1.73623	1.56596	0.213
A working woman causes strain in the family	5.98307	236.63111	5.98307	1.89305	3.16055	0.078
A woman must be economically independent	**23.64529**	**158.77991**	**23.64529**	**1.27024**	**18.61483**	**0.000**
Husband and wife must share work equally	**3.79743**	**93.966335**	**3.79743**	**.75173**	**5.05158**	**0.026**
Women must stand-up for their rights	**10.41838**	**125.45563**	**10.41838**	**1.00365**	**10.38054**	**0.002**
A woman must do things which she thinks right	3.03722	157.86042	3.03722	1.26288	2.40499	0.123
Discos are no places for women	5.97622	219.37812	5.97622	1.75502	3.40520	0.067
Working women are bad housewives	5.15069	232.37687	5.15069	1.85901	2.77066	0.099
The woman as homemaker and the man as income generator is ideal	**12.94272**	**241.24626**	**12.94272**	**1.92977**	**6.70617**	**0.011**

2. 'Husband and wife must share the family work equally'
   Male heavy : 4.16
   Female heavy : 4.51
3. 'Women must stand up for their rights and assert themselves'
   Male heavy : 3.76
   Female heavy : 4.34
4. 'Woman as home-maker and man as income gene :ator is good for an ideal family'
   Male heavy : 2.53
   Female heavy : 3.67

The data on individual mean scores suggests that females put more emphasis than do males in a consistent pattern for all the four dependent variables of 'Social roles of Indian women'. Thus the hypothesis is statistically supported.

Two dependent variables in the study appeared to reflect traditional gender role attitudes of men. Female heavy viewers strongly agreed that women must be economically independent but males were undecided about it. The dilemma of male heavy viewers on the dependent variable economic independence for women implies evolving power differences in the family. On the other hand, female heavy viewers of FTP have strongly asserted this factor. This shows their quest for economic independence.

Another dependent variable on which female and male heavy viewers differed significantly was about the traditional image of an ideal Indian family in which woman is a homemaker and man is an income-generator. Male heavy viewers are undecided whereas females disagreed to it. Heavy viewing of FTP has not changed the attitude of males with regard to the traditional image of wife holding the responsibility of the family and husband for economic support. The attitude towards perceived social roles of Indian women was found to be conservative for male heavy viewers than females. It is reasonable to conclude that these differences in perceptions are the reflections of particular social roles that these boys and girls occupy within the domestic sphere. It also implies that womenfolk seem to be changing faster.

For the dependent variable, sharing of family work by both husband and wife, female heavy viewers showed greater agreement with the statement than the male heavy viewers though they also strongly agreed to it. The parameter 'woman must standup for their rights and assert themselves' is strongly accepted by both male and female heavy viewers though females more than males showed greater acceptance.

In the joint families and in families where women are not working, the division of work in the family both income-generating and household activities was clear. Due to a number of factors, the joint families gave place to nuclear families. Both husband and wife in a nuclear family have to earn if they want to lead an economically comfortable life. As a result women also started working. The working women have to perform multiple roles both in the family and outside. The changing family environment is creating new perceptions about the roles of husband and wife. Moreover, the FTP exposed viewers to a new family environment where both husband and wife are earning and also sharing the household responsibilities. This may be the reason for male heavy viewers to show their willingness to accept the household work.

WESTERN SEXUAL NORMS

Hypothesis-5

"Young heavy viewers of foreign television programmes tend to show a greater degree of acceptance of Western sexual norms than moderate and low viewers of foreign television programmes".

The homogeneity of the variance has not been violated as shown by the significant Box's M test, F (72,418161) DF = 1.13843, p = 0.198 (approx.).

Table 7.7: Results of MANOVA Test of Significant Difference Between Three Categories of Viewers of Foreign Television Programmes on the Western Sexual Norms

(N-394)

Test Name	*Value*	*Exact F*	*Hypoth. DF*	*Error DF*	*Sig. of F*
Pillai's	0.04145	1.01846	16.00	770.00	0.434
Hotelling's	0.04291	1.02720	16.00	766.00	0.425
Wilk's	0.95871	1.02285	16.00	768.00	0.429
Roy's	0.03731				

There is no significant difference between the three categories of viewers of FTP on sexual norms. Thus the hypothesis is not statistically supported.

Hypothesis-6

"Because of heavy viewing of foreign television programmes, young male viewers tend to show a greater degree of acceptance of Western sexual norms than young female viewers."

The homogeneity of the variance has not been violated as shown by the significant Box's M test, F (91,46990) DF = 1.27526, p = 0.082 (approx.).

Table 7.8: Results of MANOVA Test of Significant Difference Between Young Male and Female Heavy Viewers on the Western Sexual Norms

(*N = 126*)

Test Name	*Value*	*Exact F*	*Hypoth. DF*	*Error DF*	*Sig. of F*
Pillai's	0.27974	4.46636	10.00	115.00	0.000
Hotelling's	0.38838	4.46636	10.00	115.00	0.000
Wilk's	0.72076	4.46636	10.00	115.00	0.000
Roy's	0.27974				

Table 7.8 shows significant difference between young male and female heavy viewers on a set of dependent variables of Western sexual norms (p = 0.000). In order to determine whether young male heavy viewers show greater acceptance for Western sexual norms than female heavy viewers, mean scores were examined by using Univariate F-test and result are presented in Table 7.9.

The results in Table 7.9 indicate the significant difference on four out of ten dependent variables of western sexual norms. It includes 'programmes stimulate interest in sex', 'encourage to indulge in casual sex', 'encourage to indulge in pre and extra-marital relationship' and 'dating enhances an understanding between partners'.

1. 'Programmes stimulate interest in sex'
   Mean scores of male heavy : 3.65
   Mean scores of female heavy : 2.42

Table 7.9: Results of Univariate F-tests for Western Sexual Norms

Variables	*Hypoth. SS*	*Error SS*	*Hypoth MS*	*Error MS*	*F*	*Sig. of F*
Programmes stimulate interest in sex	**46.66756**	**185.94355**	**46.66756**	**1.49954**	**31.12115**	**0.000**
Programmes encourage to indulge in casual sex	**26.81023**	**197.54691**	**26.81023**	**1.59312**	**16.82876**	**0.000**
Programmes encourage to indulge in pre/extra-marital relationships	**12.84517**	**195.19451**	**12.84517**	**1.57415**	**8.16007**	**0.005**
Pre-marital relationships are immoral	6.60363	236.32494	6.60363	1.90585	3.46493	0.065
Extra-marital relationships are immoral	0.02622	261.27536	0.02622	2.10706	0.01245	0.911
Unnatural sexual behaviour is a blow to moral fabric	1.22771	245.97864	1.22771	1.98370	0.61890	0.433
Unnatural sexual relationship is a matter of individual choice	4.41410	221.72082	4.41410	1.78807	2.4684	0.119
A woman indulges in pre/extra-marital relationships is not accepted by society	0.00409	180.92449	0.00409	1.45907	0.00280	0.958
A man indulges in pre/extra-marital relationships is not accepted by society	0.22782	203.54996	0.22782	1.64153	0.13878	0.710
Western pattern of dating leads to better understanding	**19.56783**	**204.14645**	**19.56783**	**1.64634**	**11.88564**	**0.001**

2. 'Programmes encourage youth to indulge in casual sex'
   Mean scores of male heavy : 3.35
   Mean scores of female heavy : 2.42
3. 'Programmes encourage youth to indulge in pre-marital and extra-marital relationships'
   Mean scores of male heavy : 3.20
   Mean scores of female heavy : 2.56
4. 'Western pattern of dating leads to better understanding'
   Mean scores of male heavy : 3.66
   Mean scores of female heavy : 2.61

The results indicate that heavy viewers uniformly scored higher means than female heavy viewers for all the four dependent variables of sexual norms. Thus the hypothesis is statistically supported.

The data reveals that heavy viewing of FTP led to the acceptance of two dependent variables of Western sexual norms. Male heavy viewers tend to agree that programmes stimulate interest in sex and encourage the youth to indulge in casual sex while females disagreed. Heavy viewing of FTP is correlated with stimulating interest in sex for men. For women on other hand, a negative correlation is found between the amount of exposure to FTP and acceptance of stimulating interest in sex. Male heavy viewers are undecided about whether programmes encourage young to indulge in pre-marital/extra-marital relationship whereas females tend to disagree.

The situation in which characters indulge in either casual sex or a pre/extra-marital relations are quite different from what are prevailing in the Indian society. The male heavy viewers are undecided about it. On the other hand, female heavy viewers are found to reject these sexual relations totally. The Indian society exercises separate sex code for men and women. Moreover the society lays emphasis on virginity of unmarried women and their loyalty to husband. All these values are deeply rooted among the females and therefore they are not influenced by the sexual norms shown in FTP. They totally rejected the idea of pre/extra-marital relations.

Male heavy viewers tend to accept that Western pattern of dating leads to better understanding and females are undecided about it. It can be said from the results that heavy viewing for males is clearly associated with tendency to accept Western pattern of dating but female heavy viewers do not seem to have made up their mind about dating.

WESTERN LIFESTYLES

Hypothesis-7

"Young heavy viewers of foreign television programmes tend to show a greater degree of acceptance of Western lifestyles than moderate and low viewers of foreign television programmes."

The homogeneity of the variance has not been violated by the significant Box's M test F with (110, 359018) DF = 0.86111, p = 0.850 (approx.).

Table 7.10: Results of MANOVA Test of Significant Difference Between Three Categories of Viewers of Foreign Television Programmes on Western Lifestyles

(*N = 371*)

Test Name	*Value*	*Exact F*	*Hypoth. DF*	*Error DF*	*Sig. of F*
Pillai's	0.04754	0.87659	20.00	720.00	0.618
Hotelling's	0.04916	0.87995	20.00	716.00	0.613
Wilk's	0.95281	0.87828	20.00	718.00	0.616
Roy's	0.03839				

The MANOVA on the Western lifestyles produced statistically no significant difference. Hence the hypothesis is not supported.

Hypothesis-8

"Because of heavy viewing of foreign television programmes, young male viewers tend to show a greater degree of acceptance of Western lifestyles than young female viewers."

The homogeneity of the variance has not been violated by the significant Box's M test F with (110,359018) DF = 0.86111, p = 0.850 (approx.).

Table 7.11: Results of MANOVA Test of Significant Difference Between Young Male and Female Heavy Viewers of Foreign Television Programmes on Western Lifestyles

(N-121)

Test Name	*Value*	*Exact F*	*Hypoth. DF*	*Error DF*	*Sig. of F*
Pillai's	0.27993	4.27627	10.00	110.00	0.000
Hotelling's	0.38875	4.27627	10.00	110.00	0.000
Wilk's	0.72007	4.27627	10.00	110.00	0.000
Roy's	0.27993				

Thus MANOVA test indicates the significant difference between the young male and female heavy viewers on the dimension of the acceptance of Western lifestyles. Pillai's criterion indicated that combined dependent variables were influenced by the level of exposure of foreign television programmes ($p = 0.000$). In order to determine whether young male heavy viewers show a greater degree of acceptance of Western lifestyles than young female heavy viewers, mean scores were examined by using Univariate F-test and the results are presented in Table 7.12.

The results indicated that significant difference was found on seven out of ten dependent variables of Western lifestyles. They are: 'relate myself with characters', 'consider characters as role models', 'imitate mannerism of characters', 'imitate the behaviour of characters', 'imitate the dress designs', 'imitate the accent' and 'aspiring to travel abroad'. The means scores to identify the degree of acceptance for each dependent variable of Western lifestyles are presented below:

1. 'Relate myself with characters'
   Male heavy = 3.03
   Female heavy = 1.98
2. 'Consider characters as role models'
   Male heavy = 3.66
   Female heavy = 2.79
3. 'Imitate mannerism of characters'
   Male heavy = 3.06
   Female heavy = 2.34
4. 'Imitate the behaviour of characters'
   Male heavy = 3.19
   Female heavy = 2.15

Table 7.12: Results of Univariate F-tests for Western Lifestyles

Variables	*Hypoth. SS*	*Error SS*	*Hypoth. MS*	*Error MS*	*F*	*Sig. of F*
Relate myself with characters	33.22949	210.91927	33.22949	1.77243	18.7479	0.000
Consider characters as role models	6.86345	183.92994	6.86345	1.54563	4.44055	0.037
Imitate mannerisms	15.59680	212.84948	15.59680	1.78865	8.71987	0.004
Imitate the behaviour	32.36822	203.31773	32.36822	1.70855	18.94482	0.000
Imitate hairstyles	1.01227	255.73153	1.01227	2.14900	0.47104	0.494
Imitate dress designs	14.09079	211.23153	14.09079	1.77505	7.93823	0.006
Try foreign recipes	3.83414	244.41379	3.83414	2.05390	1.86676	0.174
Use the programme jargon	4.18335	242.06459	4.18335	2.03416	2.05655	0.154
Imitate the accent	12.016678	216.49562	12.01678	1.81929	6.60520	0.011
Aspiring to travel abroad	8.95679	244.54735	8.95679	2.05502	4.35849	0.039

5. 'Imitate the dress designs'
   Male heavy = 2.47
   Female heavy = 1.79
6. 'Imitate the accent'
   Male heavy = 2.68
   Female heavy = 2.05
7. 'Aspiring to travel abroad'
   Male heavy = 3.68
   Female heavy = 3.13

The above results show that the male heavy viewers have higher mean scores than female heavy viewers for seven dependent variables of Western lifestyles, which implies greater acceptance of Western lifestyles for males than females. Hence, the hypothesis is statistically supported. Male heavy viewers are undecided about the statement whether they relate themselves with characters in Foreign TV programmes whereas females tend to disagree. Male heavy viewers seem to consider characters in foreign programmes as role models whereas females are undecided about it. Male heavy viewers are undecided about imitating the mannerisms, behaviour, dress designs and imitating the accent of the characters shown in foreign television programmes whereas female heavy viewers disagreed. It seems that people frequently look for TV programming that is more culturally proximate to Indian habits, tastes, dress designs, etc. Male heavy viewers reacted positively and agreed that they were aspiring to travel abroad whereas females were undecided about it. On the whole, the study results suggest heavy viewing of FTP among the males has led them to consider the characters as role models and has inculcated interest in travelling abroad.

MUSIC PREFERENCES

Hypothesis-9

> "Young heavy viewers of foreign television programmes tend to show a greater degree of preference for Western music than moderate and low viewers of foreign television programmes."

The homogeneity of the variance has not been violated by the significant Box's M test (110, 359301) DF = 0.98485, p = 0.527 (approx.).

Table 7.13: Results of MANOVA Tests for Significant Difference Between Three Categories of Viewers of Foreign Television Programmes on Preferences for Western Music

(*N* = *371*)

Test Name	*Value*	*Exact F*	*Hypoth. DF*	*Error DF*	*Sig. of F*
Pillai's	0.04735	0.87289	20.00	720.00	0.623
Hotelling's	0.04915	0.87985	20.00	716.00	0.614
Wilk's	0.95291	0.87639	20.00	718.00	0.618
Roy's	0.04119				

Table 7.13 indicates the MANOVA on the Western music preferences produced no statistically significant difference between the three categories of viewers. Hence the hypothesis is not supported.

Hypothesis-10

"Because of heavy viewing of foreign television programmes, young male viewers tend to show a greater degree of preference for Western music than young female viewers".

The homogeneity of the variance has not been violated by the significant Box's M test F (91,46990) DF = 0.96100, p = 0.547 (approx.).

Table 7.14: Results of MANOVA Test of Significant Difference Between Young Male and Female Heavy Viewers of Foreign Television Programmes on Preferences for Western Music

(*N* = *129*)

Test Name	*Value*	*Exact F*	*Hypoth. DF*	*Error DF*	*Sig. of F*
Pillai's	0.14546	2.25066	9.00	119.00	0.023
Hotelling's	0.17022	2.25066	9.00	119.00	0.023
Wilk's	0.85454	2.25066	9.00	119.00	0.023
Roy's	0.14546				

Thus MANOVA test indicates the significant difference between the young male and female heavy viewers on the dimension of music preferences. Pillai's criterion indicated that combined dependent variables were influenced by the level of exposure of foreign television programme (p = 0.023). Univaritate F-test was carried out to find out the dependent variables on which young male and female heavy viewers differed significantly and results are presented in Table 7.15.

Table 7.15: Results of Univariate F-tests for Preferences for Western Music

Variables	*Hypoth. SS*	*Error SS*	*Hypoth. MS*	*Error MS*	*F*	*Sig. of F*
Western music is a mark of being modern	0.84509	245.77506	0.84509	1.93524	0.43669	0.510
Western music is necessary	0.99477	205.20678	0.99477	1.61580	0.61565	0.434
Interest is developed after watching music channels	0.16893	166.66828	0.16893	1.31235	0.12872	0.720
Helps to dance in parties	0.01694	200.46368	0.01694	1.57845	0.01073	0.918
Knowledge of Western music gives recognition	1.42069	192.30024	1.42069	1.51418	0.93826	0.335
Western music is noisy	0.30333	210.06877	0.30333	1.65408	0.18338	0.669
Leads to disinterest in Indian music	**11.70300**	**222.49855**	**11.70300**	**1.75196**	**6.67996**	**0.011**
Encourages youth to participate in discotheques	**12.76660**	**156.27215**	**12.76660**	**1.23049**	**10.37523**	**0.002**
Enjoy Western music to indigenous music	**9.45161**	**186.12978**	**9.45161**	**1.46559**	**6.44902**	**0.012**

Table 7.15 explains that the significant differences are found on three out of the nine dependent variables of music preferences, namely, 'disinterest in Indian music', 'participation in discotheques' and 'enjoy Western music to Indian music'. The mean scores are presented below:

1. 'Exposure to Western music leads to disinterest in Indian music'
   Male heavy = 2.76
   Female heavy = 2.15
2. 'Exposure to Western music encourages youth to participate in discotheques'.
   Male heavy = 3.88
   Female heavy = 3.25
3. 'Enjoy western music more than the indigenous music'.
   Male heavy = 3.09
   Female heavy = 2.54

The male heavy viewers have higher mean scores than the female heavy viewers. Hence, the hypothesis is statistically supported.

Male heavy viewers tend to agree that exposure to western music programmes encourage them to participate in discotheques whereas females are undecided. It can be concluded that music programmes on FTP inculcated interest in Western music among the heavy viewers of FTP. Western music is dance oriented. More interest in Western music tends to lead to participate in dance. This may be one of the reasons why the male heavy viewers have mentioned that heavy viewing of music programmes on foreign channels encourages the young to participate in discos. Both male and female heavy viewers are undecided about the dependent variable of exposure to Western music leads to disinterest in Indian music. Male heavy viewers are undecided when asked whether they enjoy Western music in preference to indigenous music and females disagreed with the statement.

8

What Research Has Told Me?

The basic objective of the study was to determine whether and how exposure to Foreign Television Programmes (FTP) influences the socio-cultural attitudes of Indian youth. The study intended to find out whether heavy viewing of FTP displaces existing norms and leads the young viewers to accept the western norms as they are projected in Foreign Channels. It is generally assumed that gender differences among the viewers partly determine the nature of effects of television in general and hence the study also made an attempt to see whether foreign television programmes influence the young girls and boys differently. The researcher decided to study the young viewers, as they are more vulnerable to the external influences, which include television. The average age of the viewers under the study was 20.5 years.

The term 'influence' is understood to be a broad concept. It can be studied by finding out whether television viewing has brought about certain changes in the values and behavioural patterns of the audience under study. The influence of FTP is measured in this study in terms of change in attitudes of youth towards certain variables due to their exposure to FTP.

The findings of the study have been presented in two categories:

1. Findings on descriptive analysis pertain to viewing decisions, programme and channel preferences, reasons for watching foreign television programmes, discussion of foreign television programmes with members of the family, the effect of viewing foreign television channels on the viewing of Indian channels, and changes in other activities of the respondents as a result of watching foreign television programmes besides demographic information of the respondents.
2. Findings on hypothesis testing.

Findings of the Descriptive Analysis

The following are the findings of the descriptive analysis:

The sample was fairly uniform in terms of percentage of heavy, moderate and low viewers. Similarly the number of male and female respondents in the sample was almost the same. The analysis of the sample on the basis of the parental background like education, occupation and income demonstrated that a majority of the respondents belong to more or less the same economic and educational status. The data on the respondents' fathers' education revealed that a majority of them were graduates (52.67%). The second largest group had only high-school education (25.06%). In the case of respondents' mothers' education, mothers of more than half of the respondents (54.61%) had only high-school education. The second largest group consisted of graduates (23.50%). The percentage of fathers having post-graduate or professional qualification was 11 and 7 per cent respectively, whereas in the case of mothers the percentages were 5 and 1 in that order.

The analysis of the association between the parents' education and level of viewing revealed that the percentage of heavy viewers was less in the families in which either of the parents was a post-graduate. Though this result is not quite prominent in terms of the number of respondents, it indicates an association between the parents' education and level of viewing. However, there seems to be hardly any association between the parents' occupational and income levels and level of viewing of the respondents. This may be because the study was conducted in the first decade of the entry of FTP into India when the FTP was a novelty and parents were unaware of their nature and likely impact. Therefore, they did not probably exercise any control on the children's viewing of FTP. As reported in Table 5.19 it was found that in the majority of families under study no control was exercised on who should operate the television. Such a finding supports this interpretation.

Anxiety is expressed on many platforms that audience will lose interest in locally produced programmes after they are exposed to a variety of information and entertainment programmes on foreign channels. This apprehension was partially supported by the findings in the study. Although half of both male and female respondents reported that they were looking for both information and entertainment, heavy viewers preferred entertainment-oriented programmes to information-based programmes. In the sample, 43 per cent of the respondents said that the duration of the viewing of Indian channels has decreased after they started watching FTP. The impact is found to be more pronounced in the case of male viewers (50.46%) than the female viewers (35.50%). Fifty per cent of the female respondents mentioned that the duration of the viewing of Indian channels remained unaffected even after watching FTP. Among the total respondents, 73 per cent of heavy viewers, 35.20 per cent of moderate viewers and 41.06% per cent of low viewers reported decreased viewing of the Indian channels. Thus heavy viewing corresponds with decreased viewing of the Indian television channels.

The respondents were asked to mark their choice if they were to have either only foreign channels or only Indian channels on their cable television. Again nearly three-fourth of the male respondents preferred foreign channels, which is a higher proportion than that of the female respondents (58.29%). There is also a significant association between the level of viewing of respondents and their preference for FTP. Three-fourth of the heavy viewers preferred foreign channels, which is a higher proportion than that of the moderate (64.95%) and low (51.77%) viewers. In a similar way, preference for Indian channels was found to be higher among the low (48.23%) viewers when compared with the moderate (35.04%) and heavy (23.39%) viewers. The results support the cultural imperialism theory with regard to drawing attention of the audience in favour of foreign channels.

The study also supports the argument that men and women generally differ in their reactions to the television messages. Differences in the priorities of watching various kinds of programmes were found between male and female viewers. The male respondents mentioned news as their first choice followed by sports and feature films whereas female respondents indicated equal preference for news and music, which were followed by serials and feature films equally. In an earlier study conducted in the U.K., Morley (1988) found an association between audience gender and the type of programme preferred by them. Men favoured factual programmes and sports, and women preferred fictional, romance and local news in that order. In another study, in Nigeria, Hornig (1993) found that men ranked news, sports and music in that order whereas women ranked news in the first place followed by soap operas and music.

Monitoring and analysis of audience discussions on television messages reveals a number of factors about the respondents such as, how they understand and interpret the messages, what pleasures they derive from them and how they use them. In the present study, a question was posed to the respondents whether they discussed these programmes with family members. In the sample, 46.75 per cent of both male and female respondents revealed that they always discussed the FTP with other family members. As pointed out by Yadava and Reddy (1988), TV viewing in Indian families is more of a social activity than a private one. Moreover, not more than 2 per cent of the Indian families have two or more TV sets in the house. The viewers are bound to pass comments on or discuss the programmes while watching them. Among the respondents who discussed programmes, the percentage of female respondents (54.82%) was larger than that of the male respondents (39.65%). This finding also corresponds with the findings of the previous study by Morley (1988) where he observed that women talked more about television than men did. In the present study, however, no association was found between the level of viewing and respondents discussing FTP with members of the family.

How the audience understood and interpreted the programmes and how they used them was not directly observed in the present study. But the data about attitudes of the audience indirectly reveals them.

The data on programme decisions reveals existing power relations in the Indian family. About 58 per cent of the respondents were found to claim that there was no control of any specific member of the family on programme decisions. In the case of remaining 182 respondents (42%) it was the father or brother or the male respondent himself was making the programme decision and whose number (84) is almost double that of the mothers, sisters and the female respondents put together (45). It implies that male members exercised the programme decisions more often than female members. This finding is similar to the finding of the studies conducted by Lull (1982) and Morley (1988) through indepth interviews. Lull found that fathers most often control selection of television programmes in United States. Morley made the same observation when he pointed out that none of the women respondents controlled the remote control regularly.

Findings of Hypotheses Testing

The major findings of hypotheses testing are presented under various headings pertaining to the dependent variables used.

Western Family Norms

The dependent variable 'Western family norms' was operationalised into 17 components: attitudes towards decision by father but not by mother, mother to be consulted in decision-making, young people must have a say in career decisions, economic dependence of the young on their parents, the young should be financially independent, obeying elders, using polite language while arguing with parents, taking care of parents in their old age, opinions on self-choice, arranged and legal marriages, opinions on marriage rituals, nuclear family and living together without marriage.

The first hypothesis stated that young heavy viewers of FTP tended to show a greater degree of acceptance of Western family norms than moderate and low viewers. The data analysed by MANOVA produced statistically no significant difference among the three categories of viewers. So we have to conclude that the pattern of viewing, whether heavy, moderate or low, does not make any difference with regards to the acceptance of Western family norms among young viewers of FTP.

The second hypothesis under family norms claimed that young male viewers showed a greater degree of acceptance of Western family norms than young female heavy viewers. The statistical analysis of data partially supported this hypothesis. A significant difference was found between young male and female heavy viewers on two out of the seventeen dependent variables of Western family norms, *i.e.* 'mothers are to be consulted in decision-making process in the family' and 'self-choice marriages last longer'. The female heavy viewers showed a greater acceptance for the mothers' involvement in decision-making whereas male heavy viewers endorsed opinion that 'self-choice marriages last longer than arranged marriages'.

The mean scores indicated a noticeable change towards Westernisation among male heavy viewers as they showed a greater agreement with self-choice marriages whereas young females were found to be undecided. In Indian families, the parents generally take decisions about marriage and young women enjoy less freedom than men in this matter. In spite of heavy exposure to FTP in which love marriages are common, the female viewers could not decide on the type of marriage they preferred. It suggests that in the case of marriages decisions, in spite of heavy viewing of FTP, family exercise a greater control on girls than on boys.

Another dependent variable was mother's involvement in the decision-making process in the family. Though both young male and female heavy viewers strongly agreed with the proposition, the mean scores indicated that female viewers put more emphasis on mother's consultation in the decision-making process than males. Women's involvement in the decision-making process in the family pertains to a number of issues like financial matters, education and marriage of children and other family related matters. India being a patriarchal society, consultation with girls in the family decisions is minimal. Girls watching FTP are now exposed to different kinds of family patterns where a woman enjoys more freedom. This might have created a stronger desire among them for women's involvement in the family matters, which was reflected in their responses under study.

Western Social Roles for Indian Women

The acceptance of Western social roles for Indian women was measured through 13 statements which included opinions on career for women, economic independence, sharing of family work by both husband and wife, assertion by women of their own rights, opinions on the working women and about the image of an ideal family. Two hypotheses were developed.

The first hypothesis assumed that young heavy viewers of FTP showed a greater degree of acceptance of Western social roles for Indian women than moderate and low viewers. The hypothesis is not supported as no statistically significant difference was found among the three categories of viewers. So we have to conclude that the pattern of viewing whether heavy, moderate or low does not make any difference with regard to the acceptance of Western social roles for Indian women on the part of young viewers of FTP.

The second hypothesis says that because of heavy viewing of FTP, young female viewers show a greater degree of acceptance of Western social roles for Indian women than male viewers. The mean scores implied that young female viewers more than male viewers consistently emphasised the dependent variables on which statistically significant difference was found. Hence the hypothesis is statistically supported. Statistical difference was found in the case of four out of the thirteen dependent variables, *i.e.* economic independence for women, assertion by women of their rights, sharing of household work by both husband and wife and the concept of ideal marriage where the husband is an income-generator and the wife is a homemaker.

The broad picture that emerges from the results is that men have a stereotyped image about women whereas women accept the non-traditional roles. Despite heavy viewing of FTP in which women are shown to be economically independent, male heavy viewers were found to be undecided about women's economic independence in the family and the concept of an ideal family wherein the man is an income-generator and the woman is a homemaker. Their unequivocal reluctance to accept economic independence for women can be interpreted as an attempt to hold on to the traditional power relations in the family. Money usually defines power relations in the family. Male heavy viewers do not come out openly for a change in the existing pattern of power relations in the family. On the other hand, female heavy viewers strongly supported economic independence for women and totally rejected the ideal family in which the man is a breadwinner and the woman is confined to home.

Female heavy viewers strongly agreed with the statements in the case of the other two dependent variables, namely assertion by women of their own rights and sharing of work by both husband and wife. What is interesting was that male heavy viewers also agreed with both the propositions though not as heavily as the female heavy viewers did. But the fact that they accepted the proposition implies their willingness to share household work in the daily routine of family life and accept women as independent entities who have the right to fight for their rights.

Western Sexual Norms

Acceptance of Western sexual norms was operationalised into 10 components like stimulation of interest in sex, indulging in casual sex, opinion on intra-and extra-marital relationships and dating. Out of the two hypotheses framed about acceptance of Western sexual norms, the first hypothesis tested the association between heavy viewing of FTP and acceptance of Western sexual norms. The results did not support this prediction as the hypothesis was not statistically supported.

The second hypothesis stated that because of heavy viewing of FTP, young male viewers showed a greater degree of acceptance of

Western sexual norms than female viewers do. As indicated by the mean scores, young male heavy viewers scored higher means than female veiwers and hence the hypothesis was supported statistically. The result show statistical difference in the case of four out of the nine dependent variables about Western sexual norms—'programmes stimulate interest in sex', 'encourage to indulge in casual sex, as well as pre-and extra-marital relationships' and 'dating leads to better understanding'. Young male heavy viewers agreed that watching FTP stimulates in sex because of the emphasis on romance and rapid turnover of relationships, prohibited love and skimpy clothing of women. For female viewers, on the other hand, a negative correlation was found.

The positive correlation in the case of male heavy viewers and negative correlation in the case of female heavy viewers may be interpreted as a consequence of the prevalence of different sex codes in the Indian society. Indian girls generally react within defined boundaries of sex whereas Indian boys enjoy more freedom with regard to sex norms. Similarly in the case of acceptance of dating, male heavy viewers and female heavy viewers differed in their reactions. Male heavy viewers accepted that dating leads to better understanding whereas female heavy viewers do not. Dating involves making friends with members of the opposite gender and going out with them. Moving along with men who are not relatives is not permissible for young women in general before marriage. This may be the reason why female heavy viewers reject the idea of dating.

There was a great deal of evasiveness among male viewers when asked whether FTP lead them to get involved in casual sex and pre'extra-marital relationships, whereas female heavy viewers emphatically rejected the possibility of their involvement in casual sex and pre/extra-marital relationship.

Western Lifestyles

The dependent variable 'Western lifestyle' was examined in 10 items such as 'relating to characters in programmes', 'treating them as role models' and 'imitating their mannerisms, behaviours, hairstyles, dress designs, accent, and jargon'. The question also pertained to inclination towards trying out foreign recipes and aspiring to travel abroad. Two hypotheses were developed. Hypothesis I stated that the relationship between heavy viewing of FTP leads to a greater degree of acceptance of Western lifestyles among the young viewers than low and moderate viewers. The data did not support this hypothesis. Hence, we have to conclude that heavy viewing does not influence the attitudes towards Western lifestyles to a greater extent than moderate and low viewing among the young audiences.

The second hypothesis stated that because of heavy viewing, young male viewers tended to show a greater degree of acceptance of Western lifestyles than young female viewers. The mean scores supported the proposed hypothesis. Statistically significant difference was found in the case of seven out of the ten dependent variables of Western lifestyles. They are: 'relating to characters', 'considering characters as role models', 'imitating mannerisms', behaviours, dress designs, accent and 'aspirations to travel abroad'.

A very interesting response was given by young male heavy viewers that they were undecided about relating themselves with characters in FTP but still considered them as role models. With regard to interest in travelling abroad, heavy viewing of FTP created an aspiration to undertake it in the case of men whereas female heavy viewers were undecided about it. In the Indian families, men take their own decisions and are willing to travel anywhere either for education or career. But women cannot take such decisions independently. The Indian girls' mobility is generally related to the movement of either their parents or husbands.

Music Preferences

Preference for Western music was measured on the basis of 9 statements about it. They are: 'necessity to learn Western music', 'considering Western music as a mark of modernity', 'as a help to dance in parties and in getting recognition', 'leading to disinterest in indigenous music' and encouragement to participate in discotheques. With regard to the music preferences, two hypotheses were developed.

The first hypothesis predicted that heavy viewers of FTP show a greater degree of preference for Western music than moderate and low viewers. The hypothesis was not supported, as the MANOVA produced no statistically significant difference among the three categories of viewers. The second hypothesis under music preferences assumed that because of heavy viewing of FTP young male heavy viewers showed a greater degree of preference for Western music than young female heavy viewers. The statistical analysis of the data supported this hypothesis. Male and female heavy viewers differed significantly on three out of the nine dependent variables namely exposure to Western music leading to disinterest in indigenous music, encouraging youth to participate in discotheques, and enjoying Western music more than indigenous music. Heavy male viewers of FTP said that exposure to these programmes encourages them to participate in discotheques whereas female heavy viewers were undecided. Generally pubs and discotheques normally play dance-music. The younger generation enjoys dancing to the tunes. Exposure to Western music in FTP familiarizes the young male viewers with Western music and disco culture and hence they agreed that Western music encourages the youth to participate in discotheques. But the girls do not enjoy the same degree of freedom and so get less number of opportunities to go to discotheques.

About another variable, namely whether Western music leads to disinterest in Indian music, both male and female heavy viewers were undecided. Generally these music channels telecast music videos, which include Asian models and acts that combine elements of Western music styles with indigenous culture (Banks, 1997). This may be the reason for both male and female heavy viewers for not giving a clear response. With regards to response to Western music in preference to Indian music, male heavy viewers were found to be undecided whereas female heavy viewers said that they did not prefer Western music to indigenous music.

Thus it may be observed that exposure to FTP, whether heavy, moderate or low, is not significantly related to the acceptance by young male and female viewers of Western norms projected in them.

However there was a significant difference in the way in which heavy viewing of FTP influences the male and female viewers. The difference may be attributed to the way the boys and girls are brought up, educated and treated in general in the Indian families. The nature of the influence of FTP viewing on male and female heavy viewers was also found to be significantly related to the type of the dependent variable included in the study. These findings also correspond with the observations made by Albert Bandura while discussing his Learning Theory. According to him learning occurs when the observer perceives the events or behaviours in the television and he or she feels competent in performing them. Bandura also suggested that behaviour is likely to be imitated when it is socially rewarded.

Female viewers rejected the Western norms about sex, which may be due to the fact that, in Indian society, such norms are not only not rewarded, but are, in fact, actively discouraged. However the restrictions are not so strict in the case of boys. As a result, the males were found to be more open and on the verge of accepting Western norms to a greater degree than the females.

The norms, which were endorsed by male heavy viewers of FTP, pertained to self-choice marriage, dating, going to discotheques, considering the characters in FTP as role models, stimulated interest in sex and travel aspiration. Yet with regards to images of Indian women, they continued to support stereotyped roles for women and were reluctant to accord economic independence to women. In their concept of an ideal family, the woman was found to be a homemaker and not an income-generator.

On the other hand, female heavy viewers of FTP supported non-traditional roles for women in the society, economic independence for them, sharing of household work by both husband and wife and assertion by women of their own rights. Moreover, significantly they rejected the concept of a so-called ideal family in which the woman is only a homemaker and the role of income generating is reserved for the man.

Female heavy viewers of FTP appeared to be liberal in their attitude towards Western social role for Indian women, whereas FTP viewing does not seem to make any difference in their attitudes towards self-choice marriages, dating, discotheques and other sex-related attitudes like intra and extra-marital relationships.

In the end, it may be pointed out that this study does not strongly vindicate nor demolish the theory of cultural imperialism. There is some support for the theory as pointed out earlier in the case of male viewers' attitudes towards variables dealing with self-choice marriages, dating, discotheques, stimulated interest in sex and travel aspirations. On the other hand, in the case of both male and female viewers' attitudes towards the remaining variables, the theory of cultural imperialism does not seem to find any evidence in its support.

Limitations of the Study

The empirical approach used in the study has certain inherent limitations. It treats individuals as uniform entities. As such it fails to understand the audience's subjective interpretation of television messages. That is to say, it does not take into account what the individual members of the audience make the TV programme out to be. Such understanding of how audience interpret the programme is essential to gauge the impact of foreign television programmes. The present study dealt with the influence of FTP on young students both male and female and tried to find out whether there is an association between gender, medium of instruction, parents' financial status and education and the impact of FTP. However, it did not study the impact of specific programme of FTP. It also appears from the study that had the impact of specific foreign television programme on the chosen sample over a certain period of time been quantified, more insightful results might have been obtained.

The researcher looked into the gender differences in general. If the same study had been conducted on boys and girls in the same environment where they were exposed to FTP and had their responses been collected through in-depth interviews, more valid and useful data might have become available. In the present research, the change in attitude towards acceptance of Western norms cannot be completely attributed to the FTP viewing. Most of the students had education through English medium at the school as well as the college level. The language has a strong influence and the ability to read, listen to and speak. English is related to an understanding of programming on cable. As a result, they could have absorbed some impact of Western values through academic and other books, and entertainment programmes consisting of films, music and drama. As such they might have acquired some Western values or developed a positive attitude towards them. This could have affected their television viewing and get influenced by these programmes.

Moreover, it was found that some of the words and phrases used in the questionnaire dealing with sexual norms were not clearly understood by the respondents. The researcher had noticed this during the pilot study. As a result, some words and phrases were made more explanatory in the final questionnaire. Yet while analysing the data the researcher realised that there were a few more phrases and words, which were found to be not very clear to the respondents. Words and phrases like 'dating', 'pre-/extra-marital relationships', although, very generally understood by the repondents, all their connotations and ramifications were not clearly understood. Consequently, responses of some of the respondents might have been vitiated or ill informed.

Many studies have indicated a stronger association between the viewing patterns, impact of FTP and socio-economic and educational status of the respondents. The higher the income and educational levels and the higher the preference for the foreign programmes. A majority of the respondent under study belonged to the monthly income group of 3000-8000 rupees. Their fathers were the earning members and their mothers were housewives. The sample represents the middle class youth in India and indicates their attitude towards the FTP. But the study fails to trace whether and how these socio-economic differences reflect in the influence of FTP.

Despite all these limitations the study throws light on certain important areas where further investigation may yield a deeper insight into the topic.

Suggestions for Future Research

There are a number of implications for further research arising from the present study.

The present study addressed only a few parameters for each dimension of Western norms. A detailed study may be conducted on each dependent variable and the reactions of the respondents may be observed closely. For example, research is required to be conducted on music preferences of the younger generation to find out how they react to themes in lyrics and behaviour of the models in music videos.

Similarly, an in-depth study may be undertaken to find out the respondents' attitudes to family relations projected in the FTP. Another potential area of research with regard to the impact of FTP is a comparative examination of the positive and negative values projected in foreign as well as government-owned and private Indian television channels.

There are two avenues to approach such a comparative examination. The first is textual analysis of FTP as well as programmes on official and private channels. The other is conducting field studies following the ethnographic method of research. In ethnographic approaches, the researcher can sensitively understand the complex subjective world of the television audience and how socio-cultural factors influence the audience's interpretation and internalization of television messages. Ethnographic studies in Europe, Australia and the USA have made a valuable contribution to an understanding of the audience, but a very little research is available in the Third World countries.

Bibliography

Aggarwal, V.B. (1993). Impact of cable television on social life, *Communicator*, July-September, 3 : 7-12.

Agrawal, Binod C. (1999). Feeling the pulse of changing media audiences—Some methodological issues, *Media Asia*, 26 : 3 : 162-166.

Agrawal, Hema (1995). *Society, Culture and Mass Communication Sociology of Journalism*, New Delhi : Rawat Publications.

Alexis, Tan. S., *et al.* (1987). American TV in the Philippines—A test of cultural impact, *Journalism Quarterly*, 64 : 1 : 65-67.

Allport, Gordon W. (1935). In Tobia L. Worth. (ed.). (1989). *International Encyclopedia of Communications*, Vol. 4, New York: Oxford University Press.

Anderson, P.A. (1993). Quoted by William Douglas, (1996).

Andsager, Julie L. and Kimberly Roe (1999). Country music videos in country's year of the women, *Journal of Communication*, 49 : 1 : 69-82.

Babi, Fred Bobuin. (1990). The adoption of television in Cameroon and its effects on youth, *Dissertation Abstracts International*, 50 : 7 : 2010-A.

Ball-Rokeach, Sandra J. and Melvin L. DeFleur. (1976). A dependency model of mass media effects, *Journal of Communication Research*, 12 : 4 : 485-510.

Bandura, Albert. (1973). *Aggression : A Social Learning Analysis*, Englewood Cliffs, N.J. : Prentice-Hall.

Bandura, Albert (1977). *Social Learning Theory*, Englewood Cliffs, N.J. : Prentice-Hall.

Banks, Jack (1997). MTV and the globalization of Pop culture, *Gazette*, 59 : 1 : 43-60.

Bem, Sandra Lipsitz (1993). *Lenses of gender—Transforming the Debate on Sexual Inequality*. New Haven, CT : Yale University Press.

Berry, Gordon L. and Joy Keiko Asamen. (eds.). (1993). *Children and Television—Images in a Changing Socio-cultural World.* London : Sage.

Beteille, Andre. (1999). *The family and the reproduction of inequality economics in the family,* In Patricia Uberoi. (ed.). (1999).

Bhatt, S.C. (1994). *Satellite invasion of India.* New Delhi : Gyan Publishing.

Bonafadelli, Heiniz (1986). Uses and functions of mass media for Swiss youth—An empirical study, *Gazette*, 37 : 6-18.

Botta, Renee A. (1999). Television images and adolescent girls' body image disturbance, *Journal of Communication*, 49 : 2 : 22-41.

Broadcasting Bill : Issues and Perspectives (1996). Ministry of Information and Broadcasting, In Monroe E. Price and Stefaan G. Verhulst, (eds.). (1998).

Brown, Jane D. (1988). Quoted by Abhijit Sen. (1993).

Brown, Jane D. and Kennith Campbell. (1986). Race and gender in music videos—The same beat but a different drummer, *Journal of Communication*, 36 : 1 : 94-106.

Brown, Jane D., *et al.* (1996). The influence of new media and family structure on young adolescents' TV and Radio use, *Communication Research*, 17 : 1 : 65-82.

Cable Television Networks (Regulation) Bill, 1993. In S.C. Bhatt. (1994).

Cantor, M.G. and J.M. Cantor (1992). *Prime-time Television—Content and Control*, Newbury Park, CA : Sage.

Coldevin, Gary O. (1979). Satellite television and cultural replacement among Canadian Eskimos—Adults and adolescents compared, *Communication Research*, 6 : 2 : 115-134.

Comstock, J. and K. Strzyzewski (1990). Interpersonal interaction on television—Family conflict and jealously on prime time, *Journal of Broadcasting and Electronic Media*, 34 : 263-282.

Darschin, W. and B. Frank (1997). Tendenzen in Zuschaueverhalten. (Developments in audience behaviour). *Media Perspektiven.* 4 : 174-185.

de Vaus, D.A. (1993). *Surveys in Social Research*, London : UCL Press Ltd.

DeFleur, Melvin L. and Sandra J. Ball-Rokeach (1989). *Theories of Mass Communication*, New York : Longman.

Desai, M.V. (1992). Cable TV what does the United States experience suggest? Paper presented at International Seminar on Satellite and Cable TV opportunities and challenges, organised by Indian Institute of Mass Communication and Friedrich Ebert Stiftung, New Delhi, Nov. 17-18.

Dittmar, M.L. (1994). Relation among depression, gender and television viewing of college students, *Journal of Social Behaviour and Personality*, 9 : 317-328.

Douglas, William (1996). The fall from grace? The modern family on television, *Communication Research*, 23 : 6 : 675-702.

Douglas, William and Beth M. Olson (1996). Subversion of the American family? An examination of children and parents in television families, *Communication Research*, 23 : 1 : 73-99.

Dua, M.R. (2000). TV *vs.* Print—The debate continues, *Vidura*, 37 : 1 : 21-22.

Durham, Meenakshi Gigi (1999). Girls, media and the negotiation of sexuality—A study of race, class, and gender in adolescent peer groups, *Journalism and Mass Communication Quarterly*, 76 : 2 : 193-216.

Dyal, Rajeshwar (ed.) (1992). Cable TV—Glitter or gloom-public perception of and reaction to multi-channel cable TV in India. A Report of the Indian Institute of Mass Communication, New Delhi.

Eisenstadt (1972). Quoted by P.S. Nair *et al.* (1989).

Elasmar, Michel G. and John E. Hunter (1997). The impact of foreign television on a domestic audiences—A meta analysis, *Communication Year Book*, Vol. 20, New Delhi : Sage.

Elliot, Faith Robertson (1996a). *The Family—Change or Continuity?* Basingstoke, London : Macmillan.

Elliot, Faith Robertson (1996b). *Gender Family and Society*, London: Macmillan.

Feldman Harold and Feldman, Margaret (1985). *Current Controversies in Marriages and Family*, New Delhi : Sage.

Firdaus, Kharas K. (1997). Communicating across border, *Media Asia*, 24 : 3 : 152-162.

French, David and Michael Richards (eds.) (1996). *Communication and Human Values—Contemporary Television—Eastern Perspective*, New Delhi : Sage.

Goldberg (1994), Quoted by K.M. Kapadia, (1995).

Goode, William J. (1987). *The Family*, New Delhi : Prentice-Hall.

Goodhardt, G.J., *et al.* (1987)—*The Television Audiences—Patterns of Viewing—An update*, England : Gower Publishing.

Goodman, I.F. (1983). Television role in family interaction, *Journal of Family Issues*, 4 : 405-424.

Goonasekera, Anura (1987). The influence of television on cultural values with special reference to third world countries, *Media Asia*, 14 : 1 : 7-12.

Goonasekera, Anura (1975). Asian viewers do not see western programmes as corrupting their culture, *Media Asia*. 22 : 4 : 217-221.

Gopal, Saksena (1996), *Cable TV in India-Changes and Challenges*. New Delhi: Vikas Publishing House.

Greenberg, Bradley S. *et al.* (1987). Quoted by Jane D. Brown *et al.* (1996).

Gupta, V.S. (1995). *Third Revolution in Indian Perspective—Contemporary Issues and Themes in Communication*, New Delhi: Concept Publishing Company.

Hagiwara, Shigeru *et al.* (1999). The reception of global TV in Asia—An assessment of its impact on local cultures, *Asian Journal of Communication*, 9 : 1 : 1-19.

Hall, Stuart (1986). Cultural studies—Two paradigms. In Richard Collins, *et al.* (eds.). (1986).

Hamelink, C. (1977). *Cultural Autonomy in Global Communication* New York : Longman.

Hansen, Anders (1998). *Mass Communication Research Methods*, London : Macmillan, p. 225.

Hansen, C.H. (1989). Quoted by Christine Hall Hansen and Walter Krygowski, (1994).

Hansen and Hansen (1990), Quoted by Christine Hall Hansen and Walter Krygowski, (1994).

Hansen, Christine Hall and Walter Krygowski (1994). Arousal—Augmented priming effects—Rock music videos and sex object schemes, *Communication Research*, 21 : 1 : 24-47.

Hareven, Tamara K. (1988). Continuity and change in the American family, In Luther S. Luedtks (ed.) (1988).

Harrison, K. and J. Cantor (1997). The relationship between media consumption and eating disorders, *Journal of Communication*, 47 : 1 : 40-67.

Hintz, K.E. (1992). Children's favourite television families—A descriptive analysis of role interactions, *Journal of Broadcasting and Electronic Media*, 36 : 443-451.

Henslin, James M. (1985). *Marriage and Family in a Changing Society*, New York : Free Press.

Hobson, Dorothy (1982). *Crossroads—The drama of soap opera*, London : Methuen.

Hornig, Susanna *et al.* (1993). New media and old inequities—Gender and media use in Nigeria, *Gazette*, 52 : 159-163.

Johnnson, Smaragdi U. (1983). Quoted by James Shanahan and Michael Morgan. 1992.

Joshi, P.C. (1985). An Indian Personality for Television—Report of the Working Group on Software for Doordarshan, New Delhi : Government of India.

Kang, Jong Geum (1989). Cultural indicators—The Korean Cultural Outlook Profile, Ph.D. Dissertation, University of Massachusetts, *Dissertation Abstracts International*, 50 : 5 : 1126-A.

Kang, Jong Geun and Michael Morgan. (1988). Culture clash-Impact of U.S. television on Korea, *Journalism Quarterly*, 65 : 2 : 431-438.

Kapadia, K.M. (1995). *Marriage and Family in India*, Bombay : Orient Books.

Karnik, Kiran (1999). Multi-channel television—Poverty amidst plenty? *Media Asia*, 26 : 2 : 94-97.

Karthigesu, Ranggasamy, (1991). U.S. television programmes and Malayasian audiences, *Media Asia*, 18 : 2 : 103-108.

Katz, E. and Tamar Liebes. (1984). Once upon a time in Dallas, *Intermedia*, 12 : 3 : 28-32.

Kost. (1996). Quoted In William Douglas. (1996).

Kuo, Yi-Wu, (1990). Television and the value systems of Taiwan's adolescents—A cultivation analysis. Ph.D. Dissertation. University of Massachusetts. *Dissertation Abstract International*, 50 : 12 : 3783A.

Kuppuswamy, B. (1972). *Social Change in India*. New Delhi : Vikas Publishing.

Landler, Mark (1994). Think globally, programme locally, *Business Week*, November, 18, 186-189.

Lavin, Michael (1991). The effect of Soviet television on Americans' perception of the Soviet Union, *Gazette*, 48 : 1 : 55-58.

Lawson, Annette (1988). Quoted by Faith Robertson Elliot. (1996b).

Lerner, D. and Wilbur Schramm. (eds.) (1967). *Communication and Change in the Developing Countries*. Honolulu : University of Hawai, East Center Press.

Lewis, J. (1991). Quoted by William Douglas. (1996).

Liebert, R.M., *et al.* (1973). *The Early Window—The Effects of Television on Children and Youth*, New York : Pergamon Press.

Liebes, Tamar and Sonia Livingstone (1994). The structure of family and romantic ties in the soap operas—An ethnographic approach, *Communication Research*, 21 : 6 : 717-741.

Lindloff T.R. and P.J. Traudt (1983). Quoted by James Lull (ed.). (1988).

Luedtks, Luther S. (ed.). (1988). *Making America—The Society and Culture of the United States*, New Delhi: Tata McGraw-Hill Publishing.

Lull, James (1980). The social uses of television, *Human Communication Research*, 6 : 197-209.

Lull, James (1982). How families select television programmes—A mass observational study, *Journal of Broadcasting*, 26 : 4 : 801-811.

Lull, James (ed.) (1988). *World Families Watch Television*, London : Sage.

Lull, James (1990). *Inside family viewing—Ethnographic Research on Television Viewing*, London : Routledge.

Lull, James and Se-Wen Sun (1988). Agent of modernization—Television and urban Chinese families. In James Lull (ed.) (1988).

Marks, J. (1996). The American Uncivil wars, U.S. News and World Report, April, 22 : 66-72.

McAnany, Emile G. and Antonio C. La Pastina. (1994). Telenovela audiences—A review and methodological critique of Latin America Research. *Communication Research*, 21 : 6 : 828-849.

McNeill. Patrick. (1988). Culture. In Patrick McNeill and Charles Towneley, (eds.). (1988).

McNeill. Patrick and Charles Towneley. (eds.). (1988). *Fundamentals of Sociology*, London : Hutchinson.

McNelly, John T. and Fausto Izcaray. (1986). International news exposure and images of nations, *Journalism Quarterly*, 63 : 3 : 546-553.

Mellman, M., *et al.* (1990). Quoted by William Douglas (1996).
Menton, G.W. and Galician (1987). A sociological approach to the pop music phenomenon—Radio and music video utilisation for expectation, motivation and satisfaction, *Popular Music and Society*. 11 : 3 : 35-37.
Min, Wang and Arvind Singhal. (1992), KeWang—A Chinese television soap opera with a message, *Gazette*, 49 : 3 : 177-192.
Modleski, T. (1982). *Loving with a vengeance—Mass Produced Fantasies for Women*, London : Methuen.
Mohammadi, A. (1997). *International Communication and Globalization—A Critical Introduction*, London : Sage.
Morley, David (1986). *Family Television—Cultural Power and Domestic Leisure*, London : Comedia.
Morley, David, (1988). Domestic relations—The framework of family viewing in Great Britain, In James Lull. (ed.). (1988).
Nair, P.S., *et al.* (1989), *Indian youth—A profile*, New Delhi : Mittal Publications.
Nanjundaiah, Shashidhar (1995), Deregulation of television broadcast in India—Cultural and informational impacts. *Asian Journal of Communication*, 5 : 71-87.
Neilson Media Research Report. (1995). Neilson Media Research News reporting—A study commissioned by ABC, July 11 : 1-3.
New York Times (1994). Quoted by Edward. S. Herman and Robert W. McChesney. (1997).
Ninan, Sevanti (1995). *Through the Magic Window—Television and Changes in India*, New Delhi : Penguin Books.
Norusis, Marija J. (1990). *SPSS—Introductory Statistics Students Guide*, Illinois: SPSS Inc.
Olson, C.L. (1976). *SPSS base system user's guide* (1990). Chicago : SPSS Inc.
Payne, D.E. and C.A. Peake. (1977). Cultural diffusion: The role of U.S. television in Iceland, *Journalism Quarterly*, 54 : 523-53.
Pendakur, Manjunath and Jyotsna Kapoor (1995). Quoted by Edward S. Herman and Robert W. McChesney. (1997).
Peterson, Cary W. (1994). In V.S. Ramachandran. (*ed.*). (1994). *Encyclopedia of Human Behaviour*, Vol. 3, New York : Academic Press.
Phekoo, Carol Anne I., *et al.* (1996). U.S. television viewing in

Trinidad—Cultural consequences on adolescents, *Gazette*, 57 : 3 : 97-110.

Price, Monroe E. and Stefaan G. Verhulst. (eds.), (1998). *Broadcasting reform in India—Media law from a global perspective*, Calcutta: Oxford University Press.

Raj, Usha (1995). DD joins global race for a share of the sky, *Indian Express*, 13th April.

Rahim, Abdur. (1994). Impact of Cable Television on television and video viewing in Hyderabad—A Survey, *Media Asia*, 21 : 1 : 15-20.

Rao, Sandhya (1999). The rural-urban dichotomy of DD's programming in India, *Gazette*, 61 : 1 : 23-37.

Rao, Sandhya and S.R. Melkote (1998), Quoted by Sandhya Rao (1999).

Reddi, Usha Vyasulu (1996). Rip Van Winkle—A story of Indian television, In David French and Michael Richards, (eds.). (1996).

Richards, Michael and David French. (1996). From global development to global culture, In David French and Michael Richards (eds.), 1996.

Rogge, Jan-Uwe and Klaus Jensen (1988). Everyday life and television in West Germany—An Empathic interpretive perspective on the family as a system, In James Lull. (ed.). (1988).

Rosenblatt, P.C. and Cunningham, R. (1976). Television watching and family tensions, *Journal of Marriage and the Family*, 38 : 1 : 105-111.

Ruben, Brent D. (1984). *Communication and Human Behaviour*, New York : Macmillan.

Rubin, Alan M. (1983). Television uses and gratifications—The interactions of viewing patterns and motivations, *Journal of Broadcasting*, 27 : 1 : 36-51.

Rubin, R.B., *et al.* (1986). Media use and meanings of music video, Journalism *Quarterly*, 63 : 353-359.

Saksena, Gopal (1996). *Television in India—Changes and Challenges*, New Delhi : Vikas Publishing House.

Schiller, Herbert I. (1969). *Mass Communication and American Empire*, Boston: Beacon Press.

Schiller, Herbert I. (1976). *Communications and Cultural Domination*, New York: M.E. Sharpe.

Schroder, Wertheim and Co. Report (1996). Quoted by Edward S. Herman and Robert W. McChesney. (1997).

Sen, Abhijit (1993). The impact of American pop culture in the third world, *Media Asia*, 20 : 4 : 208-217.

Shanahan, James and Michael Morgan (1992). Adolescents, families and television in five countries—Implications for cross-cultural educational research, *Journal of Educational Television*, 18 : 1 : 35-55.

Sherman, B.L. and Dominick, J.R. (1986). Violence and sex in music videos—Television and rock 'n' roll, *Journal of Communication*, 36 : 1 : 79-93.

Silverstone, *et al.* (1989). Quoted by Tomar Liebes and Sonia Living Stone. (1994).

Sinebare, Musawas. (1997). Quoted by Michael G. Elasmar and John E. Hunter. (1997).

Singhal, A. and Rogers, E.M. (1989). *India's Information Revolution*, New Delhi : Sage.

Sinha, Nikhil, (1998). Doordarshan, public service broadcasting and the impact of gobalisation—A short history, In Monrae E. Price and Stefaan, G. Verhulst. (eds.). (1998).

Skinner, E.C. (1984). Foreign television programme viewing and dependency—A case study of U.S. television viewing in Trinidad and Tobago, *Gazette*, 23 : 1 : 95-103.

Skill, T., *et al.* (1990). Family interactions on prime-time television—A descriptive analysis of assertive power interaction. *Journal of Broadcasting and Electronic Media*, 34 : 243-262.

Smith, Anthony (1980). *The geo-politics of information*, New York: Oxford University Press.

Smith, Tom W. (1990). The polls—A report: The sexual revolution, *Public Opinion Quarterly*, 54 : 415-435.

Statistical Abstract of the United States. (1992). Quoted by Faith Robertson Elliot. (1996b).

Straubhaar, Joseph D. and Gloria M. Viscasillas (1991). Class, genre and the regionalisation of television programming in the Dominican Republic, *Journal of Communication*, 41 : 1 : 53-69.

Surgeon Generals' Report. (1972). Quoted by Shearon A. Lowery and Melvin L. DeFleur (1995).

Tan, Alexis S. and Kultida Suarchavarat (1988). American TV and social stereotype of Americans in Thailand. *Journalism Quarterly,* 65 : 3 : 649-654.

Tan, Alexis S., *et al.* (1986). American television and social stereotypes of American in Taiwan and Mexico, *Journalism Quarterly*, 64 : 65-72.

Tan, Alexis S., *et al.* (1987). American television in the Philippines—A test of cultural impact, *Journalism Quarterly*, 64 : 1 : 65-77.

The Broadcasting Bill—Arrangement of Clauses. (1997). In Monroe E. Price and Stefaan G. Verhulst (eds.) (1997).

The Prasar Bharati (Broadcasting Corporation of India) Act. (1990). In G.S. Bhargava, (1991). *Government Media—Autonomy and After*, New Delhi: Institute of Social Sciences and Concept Publishing Co.

Thomas, Amos Owen (1994). Broadcasting policy *versus* commercial imperative—Television programming in Papua New Guinea, *Media Asia*, 21 : 1 : 7-13.

Thompson, Kenneth, (ed.). (1997). *Media and cultural regulation*, New Delhi : Sage.

Thornes, Barrie (1986). Quoted by Sue Lafky *et al.* (1986). Looking through gendered lenses—Female stereotyping in advertisements and gender role expectations, *Journalism and Mass Communication Quarterly*, 73 : 2 : 379-388.

Tomlinson, John. (1991). *Cultural imperialism*, London : Printer.

Tsai, M.K. (1970). Some effects of American TV programmes on children of Formosa, *Journal of Broadcasting*, 14 : 1-12.

Tufle, Birgitts. (1986). Television Video and adolescence-fascination—A key concept and basis for teaching, paper presented at XV Conference and General Assembly of International Association for Mass Communication Research (IAMCR), New Delhi.

Tunstall, Jermy, (1977). *The media are American*, New York : Colombia University Press.

Uberoi, Patricia, (ed.). (1999). *Family, kinship and Marriage in India*, Calcutta : Oxford University Press.

UNESCO Report (1981). *Youth in 1980*. Paris : The UNESCO Press.

UNESCO Report (1986). Quoted by Ved Prakash Gandhi (1995). *Media and communication today—Policy, training and development*, New Delhi : Kanishka Publishers.

Varis, T. (1984). The international flow of television programmes, *Journal of Communication*, 34 : 1 : 143-152.

Verma, K.K., *et al.* (1995). *Towards gender equality*, New Delhi : Common Wealth Publishers.

Vincent, R.C. *et al.* (1987). Quoted by Nancy Signorielli. (1993). In Gordon L. Berry and Joy Keiko Asamen. (eds.). (1993).

Ware, William and Michael Dupagne. (1994). Effects of U.S. television programmes on foreign audiences—A meta-analysis, *Journalism Quarterly*, 71 : 4 : 947-959.

Wellings *et al.* (1994). Quoted by Faith Robertson Elliot. (1996b).

Wells, Alan and Ernest A. Hakanen. (1991). The emotional use of popular music by adolescents, *Journalism Quarterly*, 68 : 3 : 445-446.

William, Angie., *et al.* (1997). Young people's beliefs about intergenerational communication—An initial cross-cultural comparison, *Communication Research*, 24 : 4 : 370-393.

Williams, Raymond (1977). Quoted by Richard Collins, *et al.* (eds.). (1986). *Media, culture and society—A critical reader*, London : Sage.

Yadava, J.S. and Usha V. Reddy (1988). In the midst of diversity—Television in urban Indian families, In Jams Lull (ed.). (1988).

Yu, Y. (1991). Quoted by Wang Min and Arvind Singhal (1992).

Zillman, D. (1988). Quoted by Alan Wells and Ernest A. Hakanen. (1991).

Index